DRAWING WITHOUT FEAR

DRAWING WITHOUT FEAR

ROBERT REGIS DVOŘÁK

Inkwell Press

This book is dedicated to

Mrs. Raymond F. Dvořák, my mother

Copyright © 1987 by Robert Regis Dvorak. All rights reserved. Printed in the United States of America.

No part of this publication may be reproduced in any form or by any means without the prior written permission of the publisher.

Library of Congress Cataloging-in-Publication Data

Dvorak, Robert Regis
Drawing Without Fear
Card Number: 97-093572

ISBN 0-945625-05-7

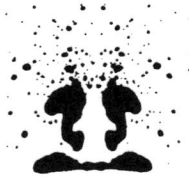
Inkwell Press
PO Box 370371
Montara, CA 94037
(888) YOU-DRAW or (888) 968-3729

CONTENTS

Introduction   vii

Illustrations and Text   1

Methods and Tools   121

Documentation of Drawings   137

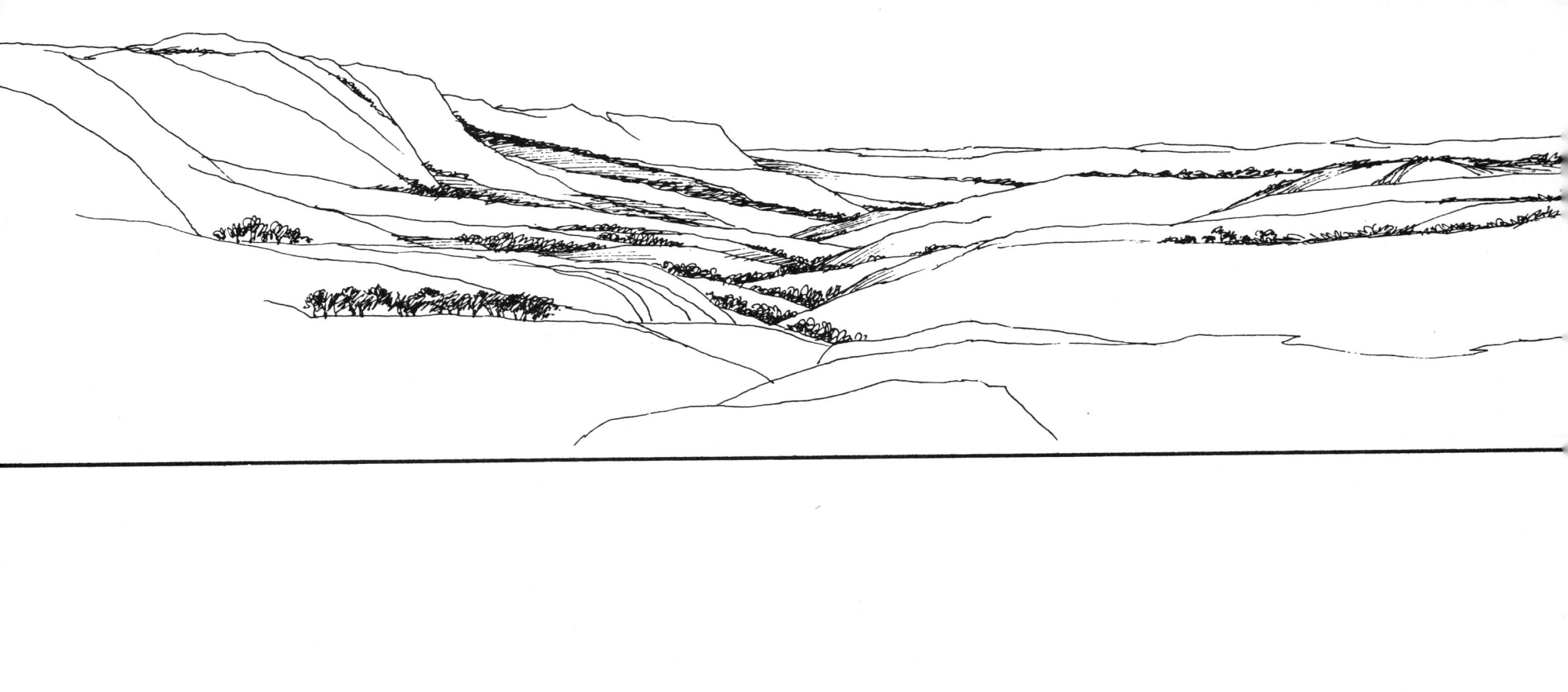

INTRODUCTION

"Art is anything you can get away with." This simple statement made by Marshall McLuhan in his book, *The Medium Is the Message,* characterizes the appropriate attitude for the creative drawing experience. Indeed, the purpose of *Drawing Without Fear* is to encourage anyone to draw anything in any way at any age. Drawing has been a simple, innocent, and natural process since the dawn of the human race. I would like to see more people enjoy this natural expression of their unique creativity. The hand-lettered loose form of this book is intended to "massage" you the reader, through the drawings and the words, to lighten your attitudes so that you can relax and enjoy the drawing experience.

The human desire to create appears to be as strong as ever. The photography industry is flourishing, and video cameras document business and recreational activities. Verbal information and word pictures occupy much of our daily activities. For most people, drawing is not necessary for survival or success. It is viewed only as play. Yet many children and most adults are intimidated by the thought of drawing anything! Their lack of self-confidence is so great that when asked if they draw, they say: "I can't draw a straight line; I don't have any drawing talent; I'm no artist; it scares me." I have found that personal satisfaction gained from drawing depends mostly on the individual's attitude and very little on the techniques learned or how much talent the individual thinks he or she has. Drawing can be practiced without any technical skills. I don't believe that certain people are born with drawing talent or that only artists can draw. Whether a person draws depends on the desire to do it.

Fear and desire are the two dominant motivators in a person's experience with drawing. Fear of failure, rejection, embarrassment, or criticism can smother desire and creativity. Eliminate fear, and desire will then spark the fire of enthusiasm, and creativity will flow. Naturally, with some self-acknowledged success, a person is willing to do more. But the definition of drawing success may have to change. Drawing anything in any way opens up possibilities.

This book offers commonsense ideas regarding the drawing process that are distilled from my experience in teaching drawing to adults, university students, and elementary school children during the past twenty years. I have also watched my young sons, Michael and David, draw with great exuberance. Of course, they have seen Dad do it and there is a natural desire to be like Dad. But I've only watched their approach to drawing. I have never given them a lesson; I have only handed them felt tip pens and brushes, laid paper in front of them, and let them create. Their excitement, concentration, and involvement as they play with lines, patterns, and compositions, changing the surface of the paper, has indicated to me that drawing is indeed a very natural and spontaneous process— easy to execute for a young, uninhibited child, often difficult for the inhibited grown-up. Though we all start life with a natural ability to be creative, we learn early what is good and bad through our role models— parents, teachers, and older children. We begin to judge, censor, analyze, and criticize. At this stage, many of us find out that drawing is not necessary for survival, and so we eventually stop. It's too risky. The fear of failure and criticism is terribly inhibiting, even for children.

Through this book I want to encourage adults and children who have stopped drawing to learn again that drawing can be a source of pleasure and satisfaction. There are no fixed rules in drawing, and anything you want to do is just fine. I would like to see you exercise your creativity with the same abandonment, relaxation, and joy of personal expression I experience when I draw.

If we have learned to be afraid of drawing, we can also learn to be unafraid. The rewards are great, the investment small. May this book inspire you to discover that you too can draw without fear.

FLIP THE CORNERS
AND WATCH THE
FACES DANCE!

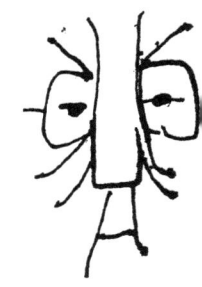

ILLUSTRATIONS AND TEXT

DRAWING

IS AN EXPERIENCE.

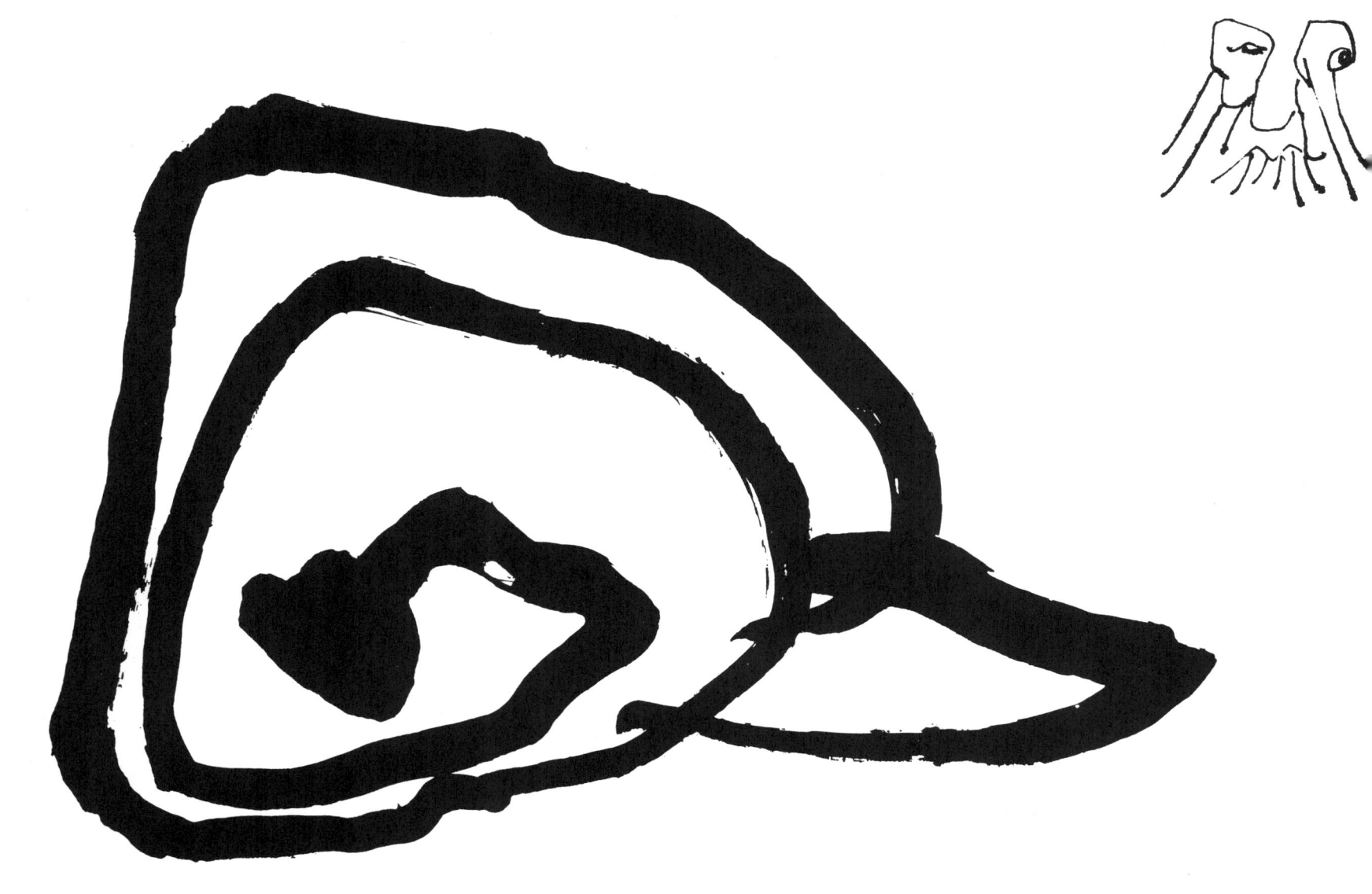

IT IS A SIMPLE PROCESS.

DRAWING IS A CREATIVE ACTIVITY.

WHEN YOU DRAW, YOU MAKE SOMETHING THAT HAS NEVER BEEN MADE BEFORE. IT CANNOT BE MADE BY ANYONE ELSE ON THIS EARTH OR IN THIS UNIVERSE.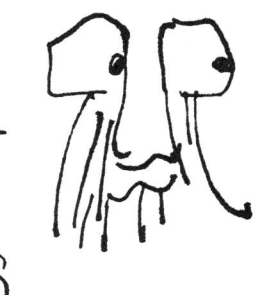

IT CAN ONLY BE MADE BY YOU.

YOU ARE THE ONLY ONE WHO CAN DO THAT DRAWING NOW. TOMORROW YOU WON'T DO THE SAME DRAWING BUT A DIFFERENT ONE.

TODAY'S DRAWING IS UNIQUE TO TODAY.

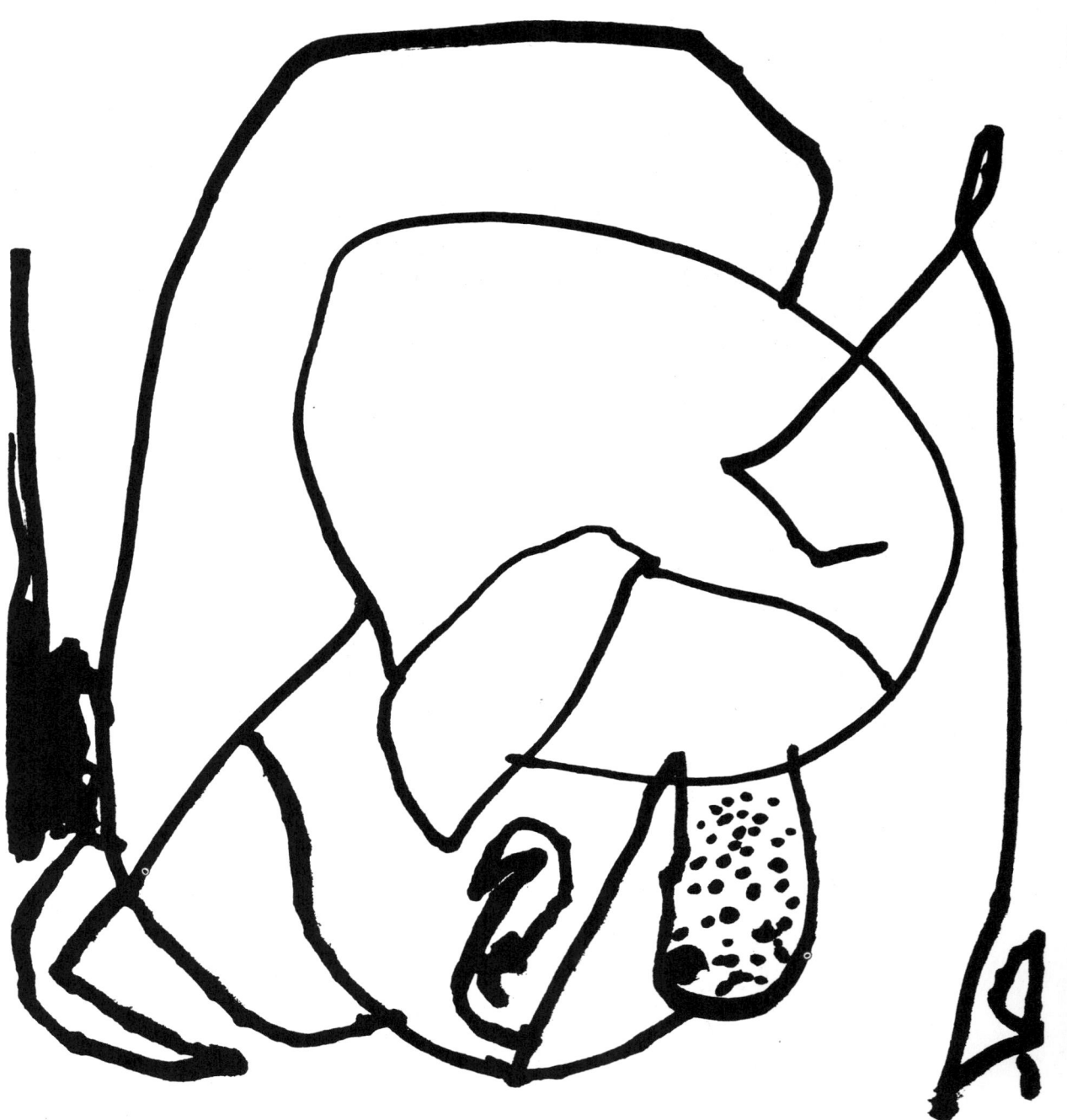

MICHAeL MOM

YOUR DRAWINGS ARE VALID BECAUSE <u>YOU</u> MADE THEM.

YOU CAN DECIDE THAT A DRAWING IS OK OR NOT. FINE! KNOW THAT YOU HAVE THE ABILITY AND THE PRIVILEGE TO MAKE THAT CHOICE. OTHER PEOPLE CANNOT MAKE IT FOR YOU. NOT AN EXPERT, A TEACHER, A FRIEND, A RELATIVE, AN ARTIST, OR A CRITIC! ONLY YOU KNOW HOW YOU FEEL ABOUT A DRAWING.

OTHER PEOPLE MAY TELL YOU HOW THEY FEEL ABOUT YOUR DRAWING. THEY MAY LIKE IT OR DISLIKE IT. IT MAY REMIND THEM OF SOMETHING OR SOMEONE.

YOUR DRAWING MAY MAKE ANOTHER FEEL SILLY SAD BORED ANGRY PROUD SCARED SURPRISED WONDERFUL OR ANY OTHER EMOTION.

OTHER PEOPLE MAY JUDGE YOUR DRAWINGS. PEOPLE LIKE TO GIVE THEIR OPINIONS. WHEN THEY DO, IT MAKES THEM FEEL IMPORTANT. PEOPLE WHO DON'T DRAW LIKE TO EXERCISE THEIR CREATIVITY TOO. SOMETIMES THEY DO IT WITH THEIR WORDS.

WHEN YOU DO A DRAWING THAT DOESN'T PLEASE YOU...

THROW IT AWAY, OR WORK ON IT UNTIL YOU DO LIKE IT,

OR PUT IT AWAY FOR A RAINY DAY, OR HIDE IT AND WORK ON IT ANOTHER TIME.

IT IS ALL RIGHT TO KEEP YOUR DRAWINGS TO YOURSELF... TO LOOK AT THEM ONLY BY YOURSELF.

WHEN YOU DRAW YOU SEE IN A SPECIAL WAY. YOU SEE WITHOUT WORDS. WORDS CAN GET IN THE WAY OF THIS DIRECT METHOD OF SEEING.

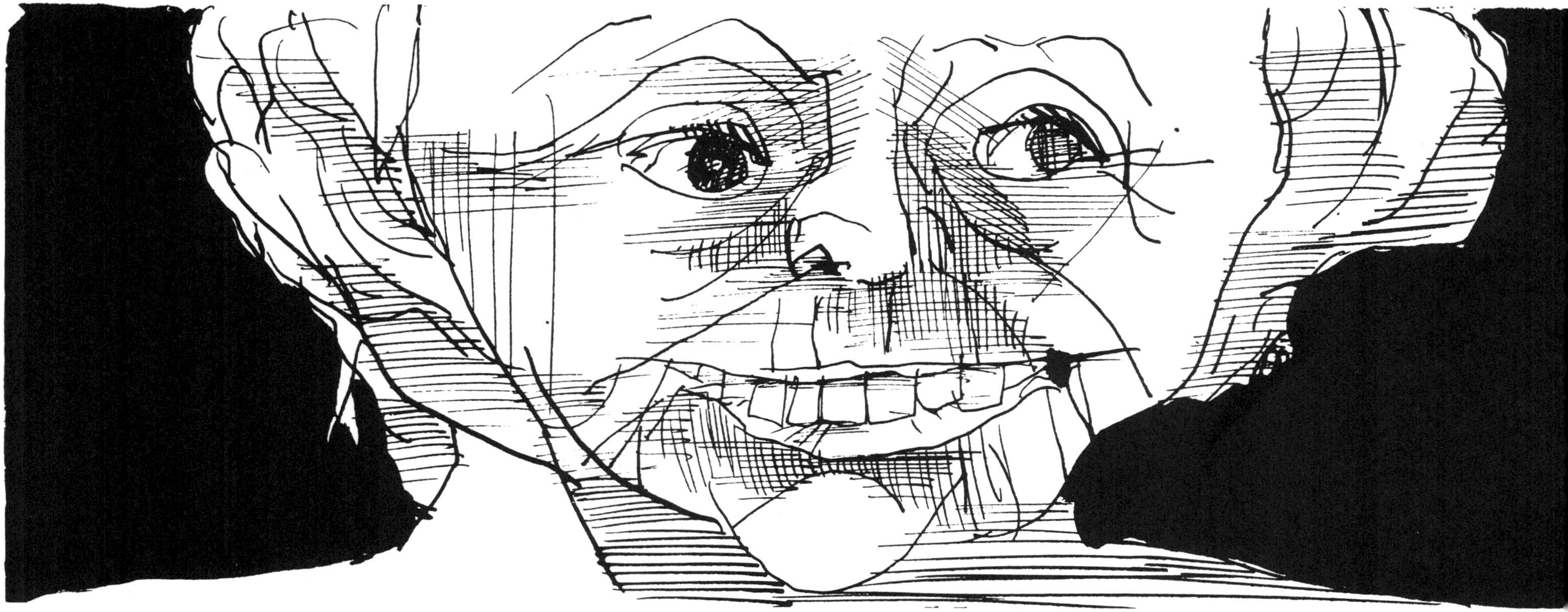

TALKING AND DRAWING AT THE SAME TIME CAN INTERRUPT THIS SPECIAL WAY OF SEEING.

WHEN YOU DRAW YOU MUST LOOK — CAREFULLY, THOROUGHLY, DELIBERATELY.

PLEASURE ENHANCES CREATIVITY. IT IS A PLEASURE TO LOOK, TO SEE. IT IS A PLEASURE TO DRAW. IT IS A PLEASURE TO CREATE SOMETHING NEW.

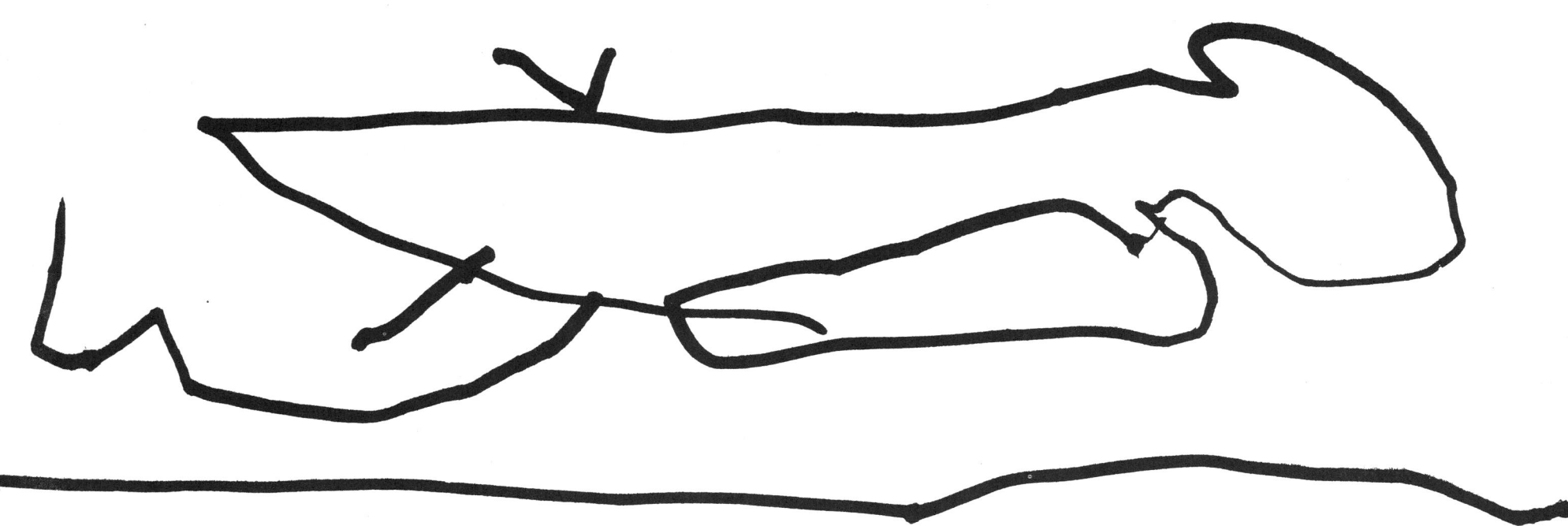

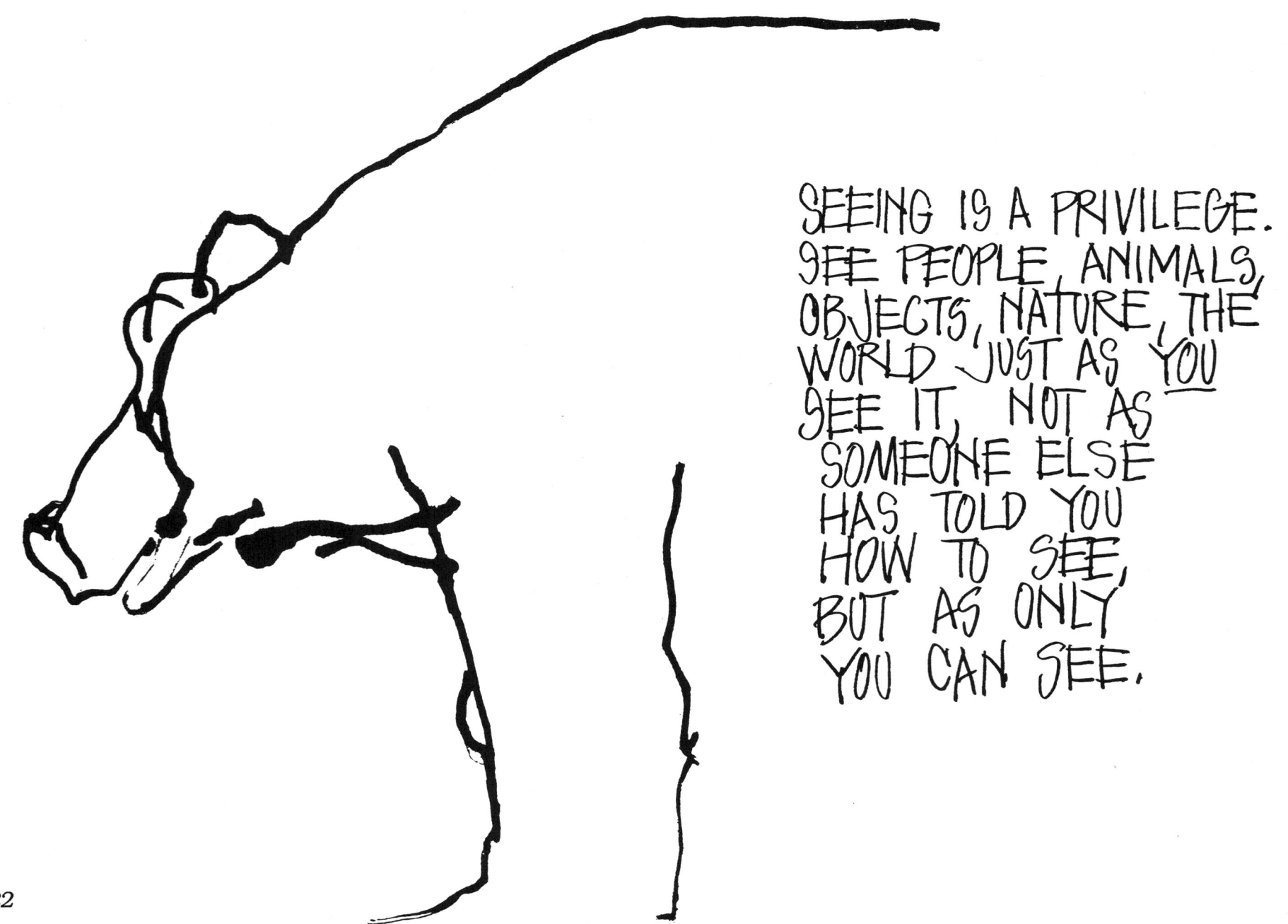

ONLY YOU CAN DISCOVER HOW TO DRAW YOUR WAY. YOU KNOW THAT INSIDE YOU, EVEN IF YOU THINK THAT YOU DON'T. IF YOU WANT TO FIND OUT WHAT WAY IS YOUR WAY, ALL YOU HAVE TO DO IS PICK UP A PEN...

AND DRAW...

AND DRAW
AND DRAW
AND DRAW
AND DRAW....

YOU MAY DRAW ANYTHING—IN ANY WAY YOU WISH.

YOU CAN MAKE YOUR OWN RULES. BUT YOU DON'T NEED RULES TO DRAW, AND YOU DON'T NEED A SPECIAL TALENT.

IN ORDER TO DRAW, JUST FIND A WAY TO MAKE LINES OR MARKS. YOU CAN EVEN HOLD THE BRUSH OR PEN WITH YOUR TOES OR WITH YOUR TEETH IF YOU LIKE.

OR YOU CAN DRAW WITH YOUR EYES CLOSED.

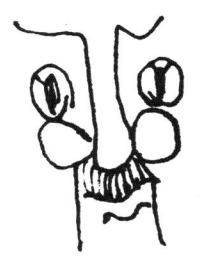

YOU CAN DRAW YOUR INNER WORLD—
THE WORLD OF YOUR IMAGINATION...

OR YOU CAN DRAW YOUR OUTER WORLD — THE PEOPLE, OBJECTS, AND SITUATIONS THAT SURROUND YOU.

YOU CAN MAKE SIMPLE DRAWINGS...

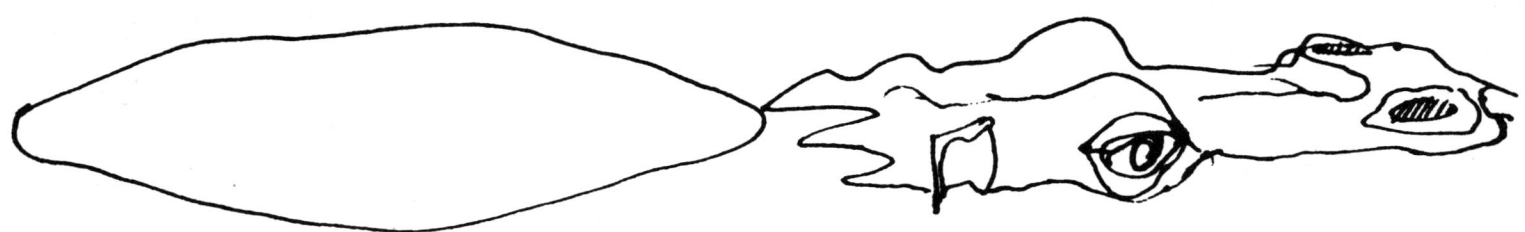

OR VERY
DETAILED
DRAWINGS.

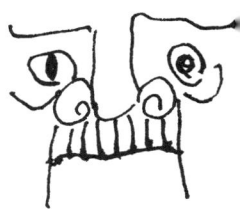

OR GROWN-UP-LIKE DRAWINGS.

YOU CAN MAKE REALISTIC DRAWINGS...

OR YOU CAN FOLD THE PAPER AND MAKE INK BLOT DRAWINGS.

YOU CAN DRAW WITH A BRUSH.

YOU CAN DRAW WITH FELT TIP PENS.

YOU CAN DRAW WITH A "DRY" BRUSH

YOU CAN DRAW WITH A "WET" BRUSH.

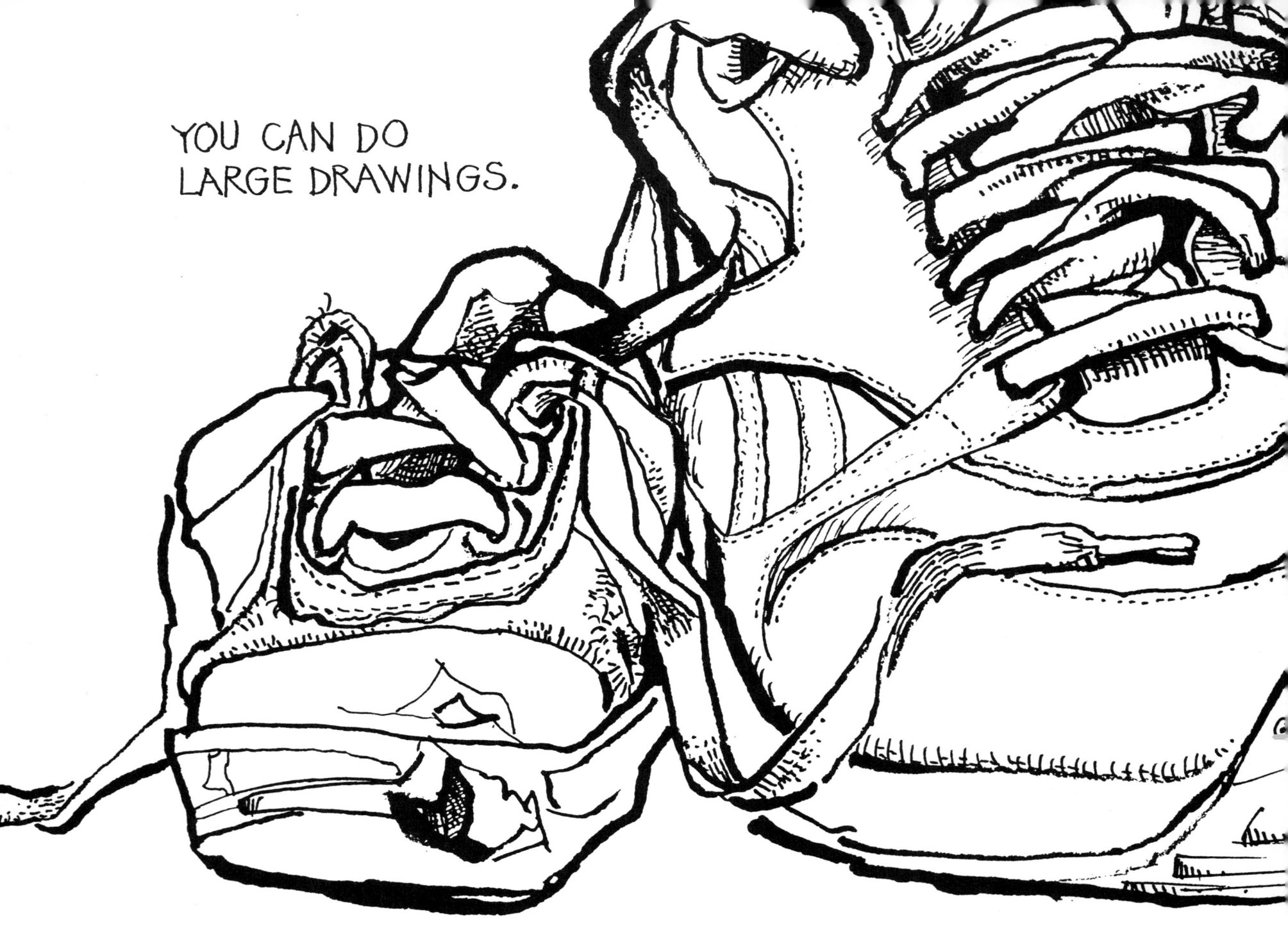

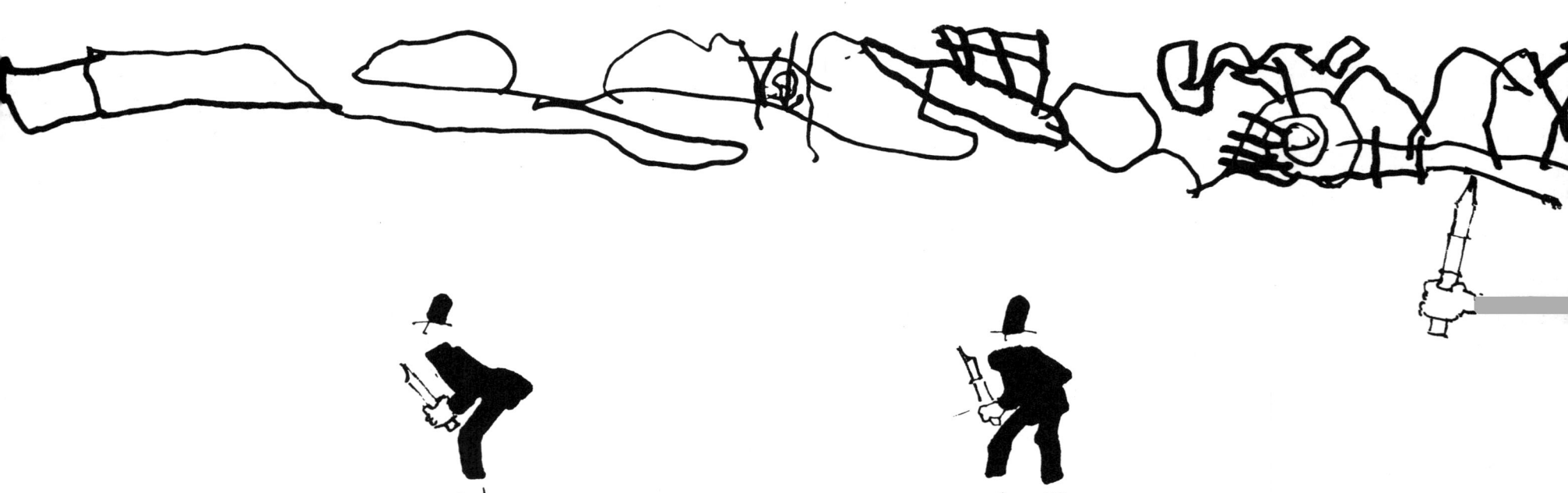

YOU CAN MAKE LONG DRAWINGS.

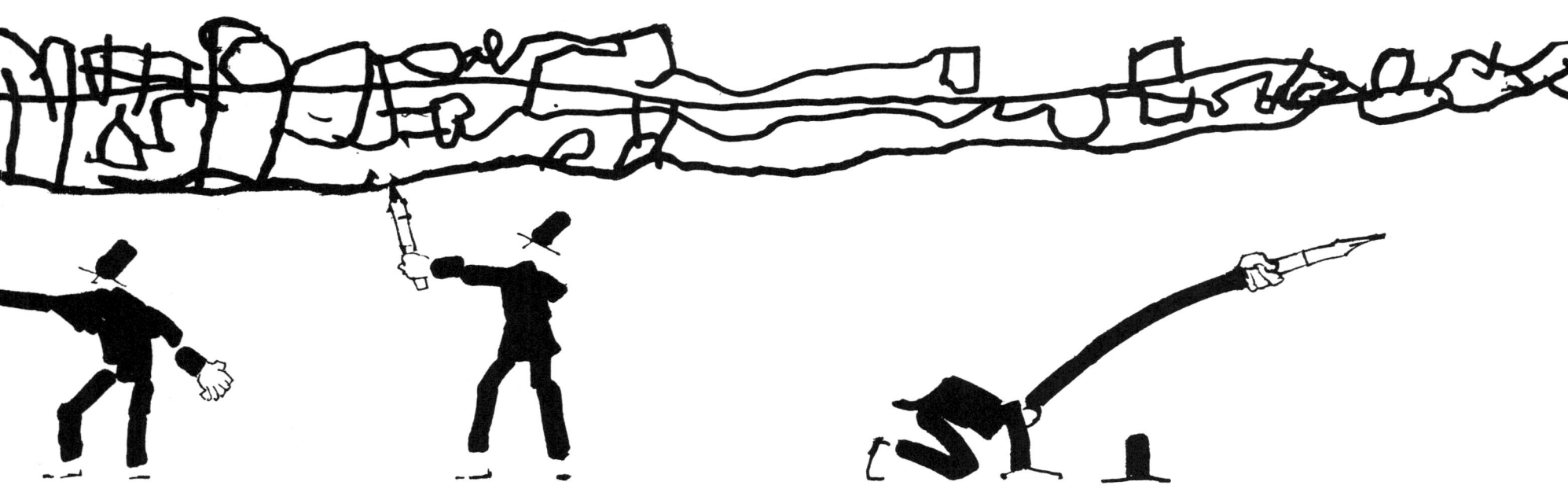

OR YOU CAN MAKE SMALL DRAWINGS.

YOU CAN DO SMALL
DRAWINGS OF
BIG THINGS,

YOU CAN MAKE LARGE DRAWINGS OF SMALL THINGS...

OR VERY TINY
DRAWINGS.

YOU CAN DRAW ANYTHING YOU LIKE. IT IS MOST EXCITING TO DRAW THINGS THAT INTEREST YOU. SOMETIMES DOING THIS WILL HELP YOU LEARN MORE ABOUT THOSE THINGS— THE WAY THEY GO TOGETHER THE WAY THINGS ARE ORGANIZED.

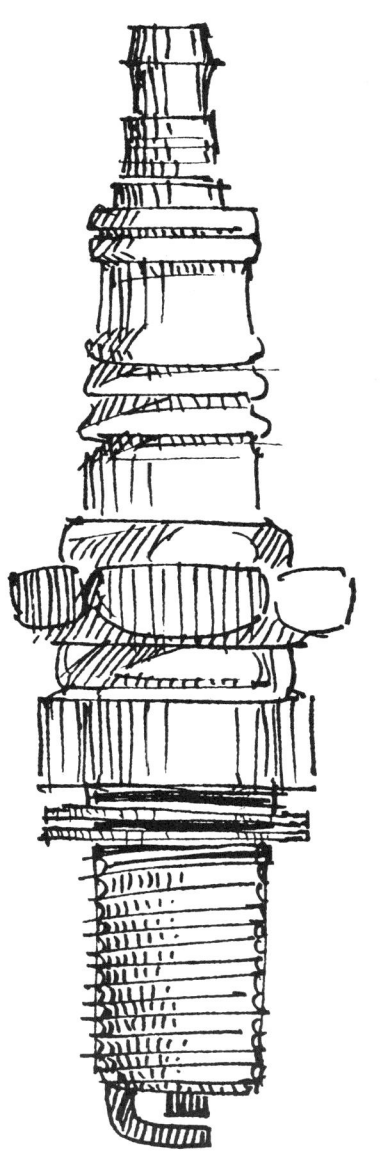

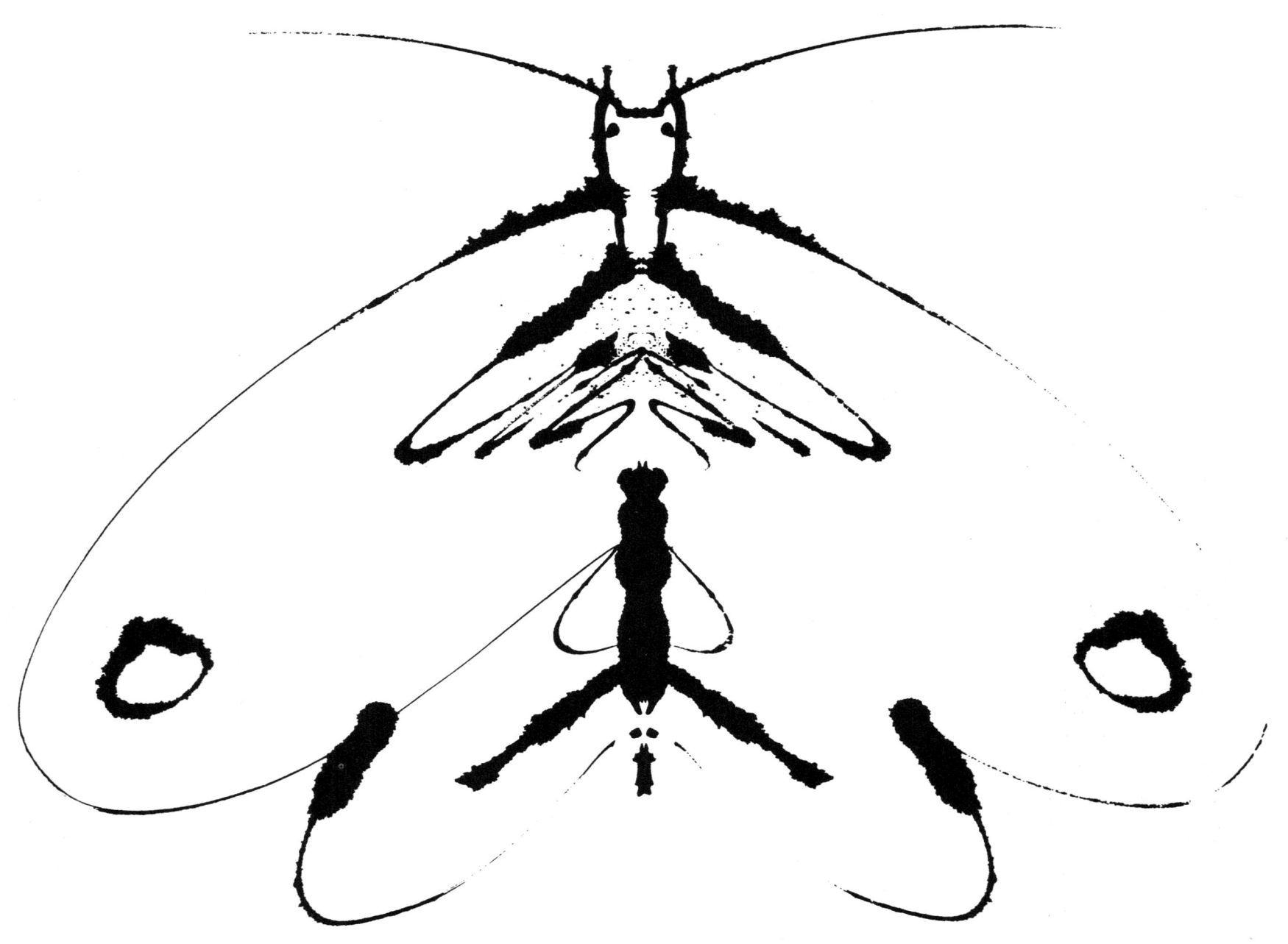

IT IS ALSO FUN TO DRAW FROM YOUR IMAGINATION.

YOU CAN DRAW STORIES.

YOU CAN DRAW PLACES THAT YOU VISIT,

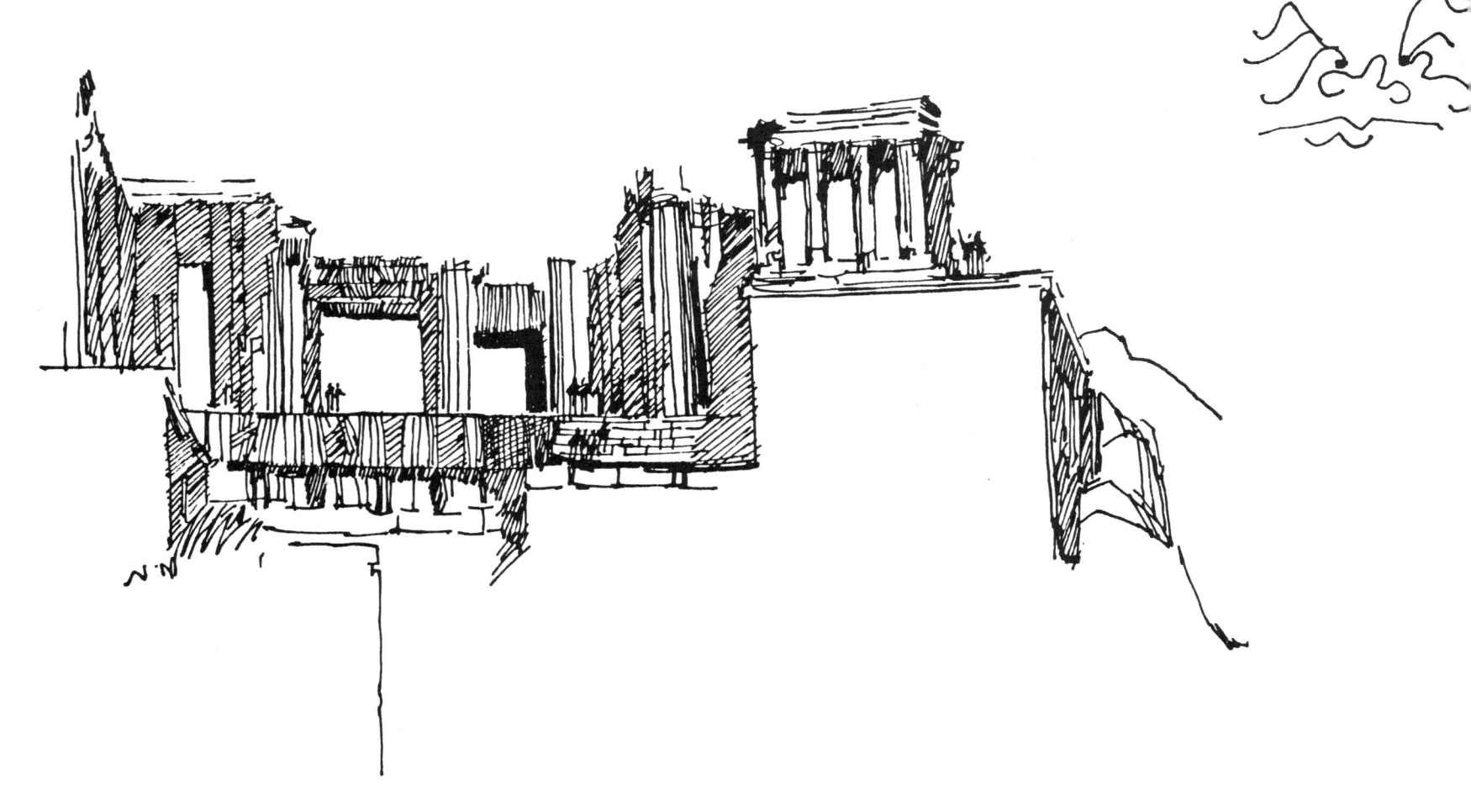

OR PLACES THAT YOU WOULD LIKE TO VISIT.

YOU CAN DRAW FROM THE WORLD AROUND YOU.

DRAW WHAT
YOU SEE
EVERY DAY.

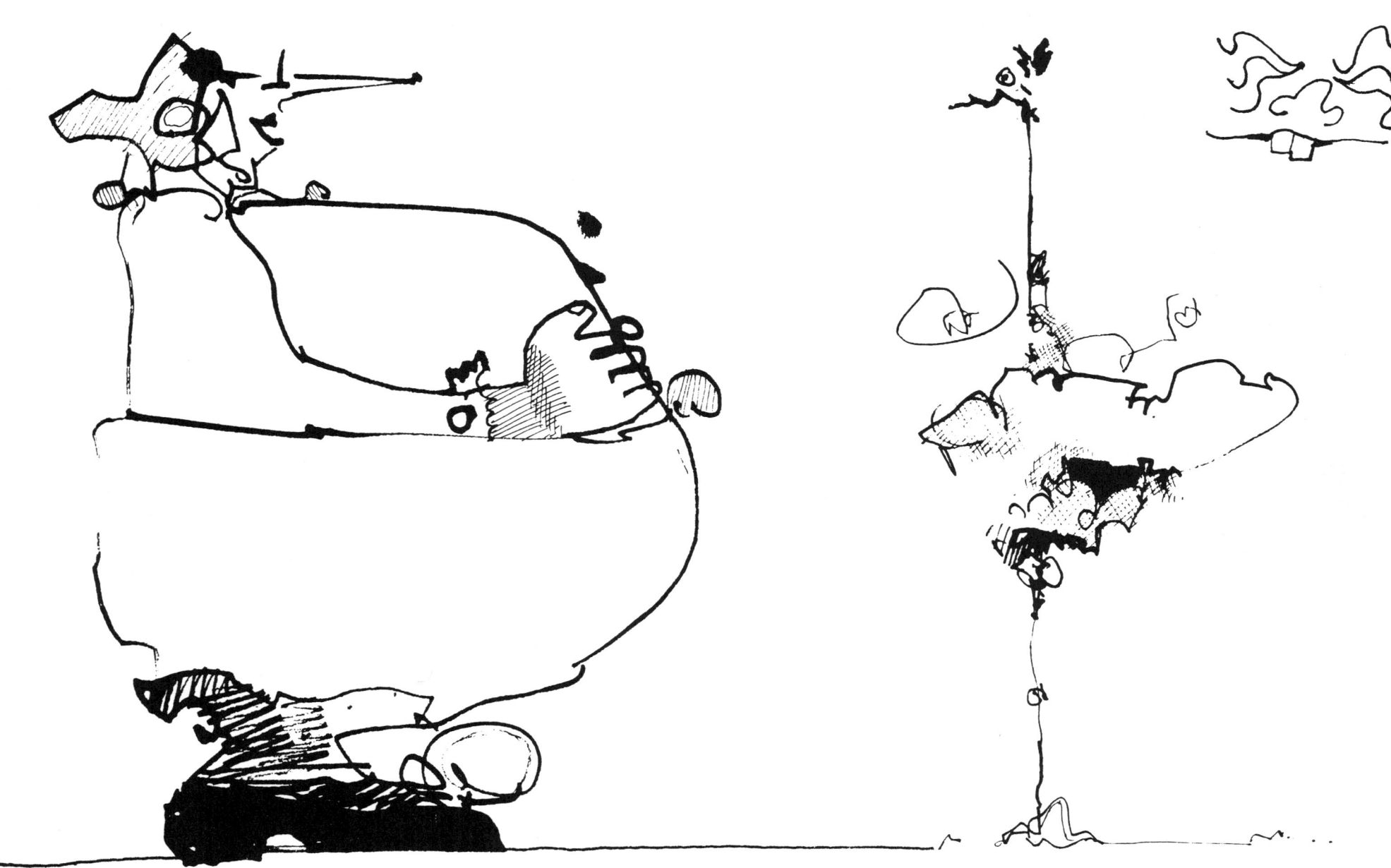

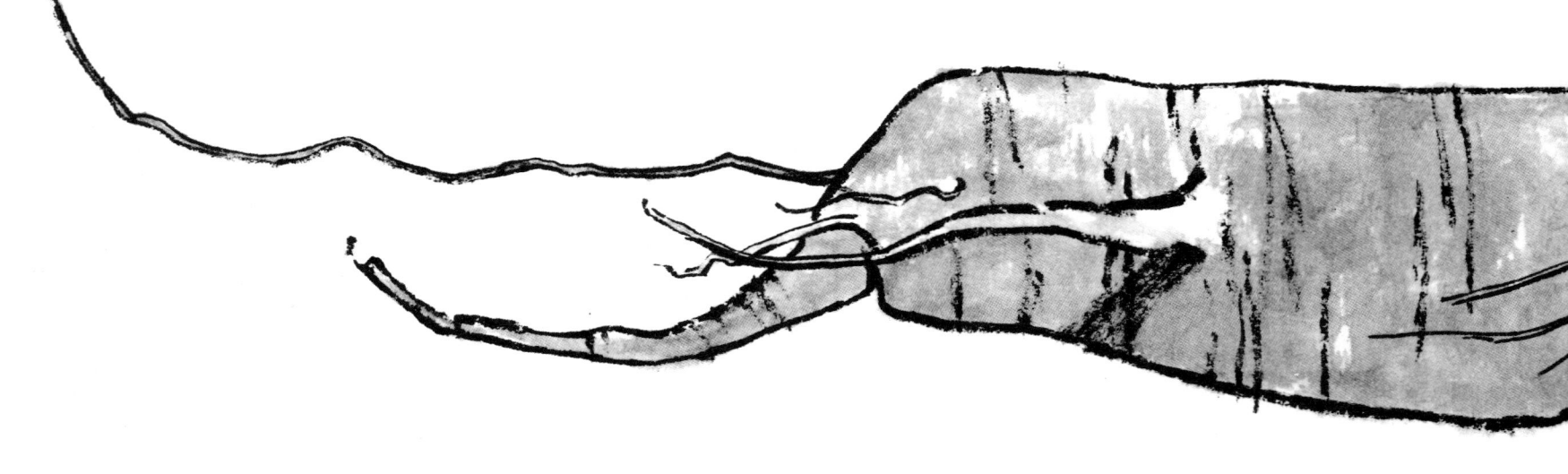

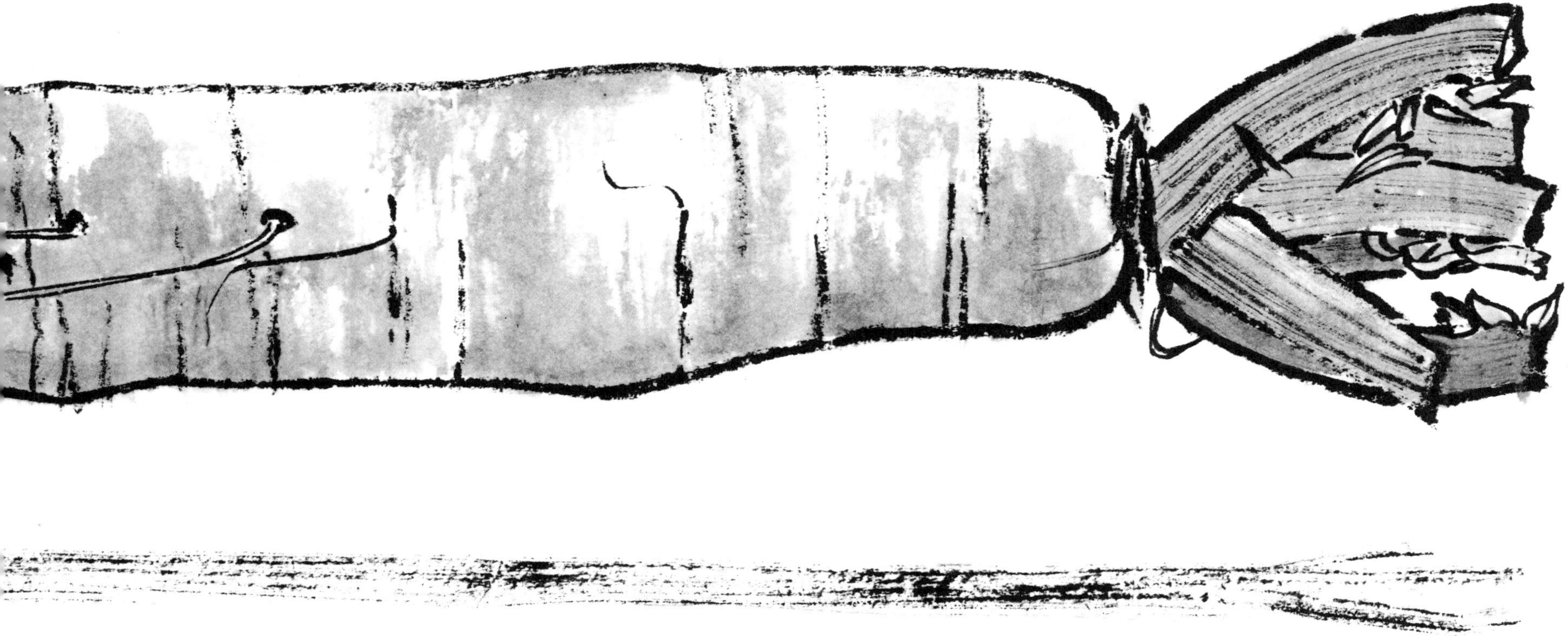

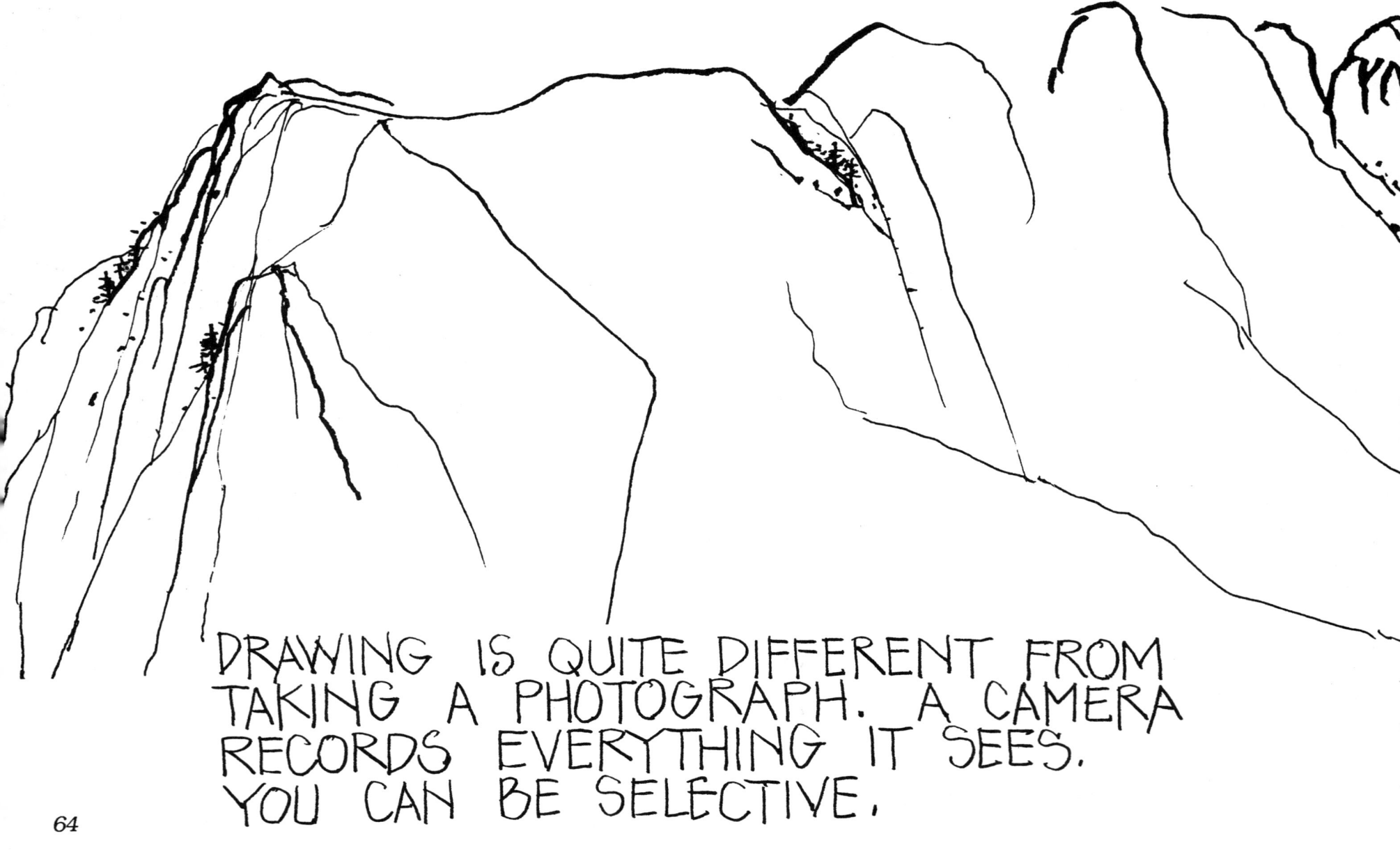

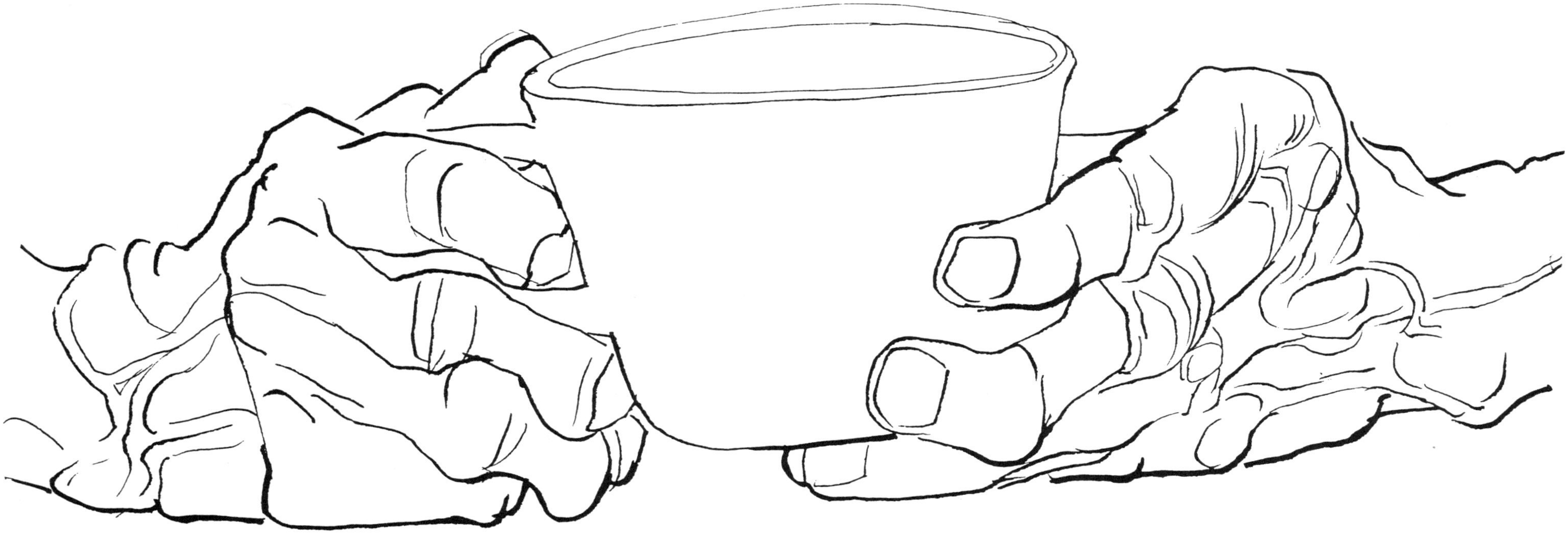

DRAWING IS A VERY PERSONAL ACTIVITY.

A DRAWING TELLS ABOUT THE DRAWER'S EXPERIENCE. IT SHOWS THE CREATIVITY OF THE DRAWER.
A DRAWING IS A RECORD OF THE WAY THAT PERSON'S HAND MOVED WHILE HOLDING THE DRAWING INSTRUMENT— OF HOW THAT PERSON WAS FEELING OR THINKING... OR BEING.

YOU MAY CHOOSE TO BE LOOSE AND CAREFREE.

YOU MAY DRAW WITH VERY STRICT RULES AND CAREFUL DISCIPLINE.

YOU MAY DRAW WITH FREEDOM AND ABANDON.

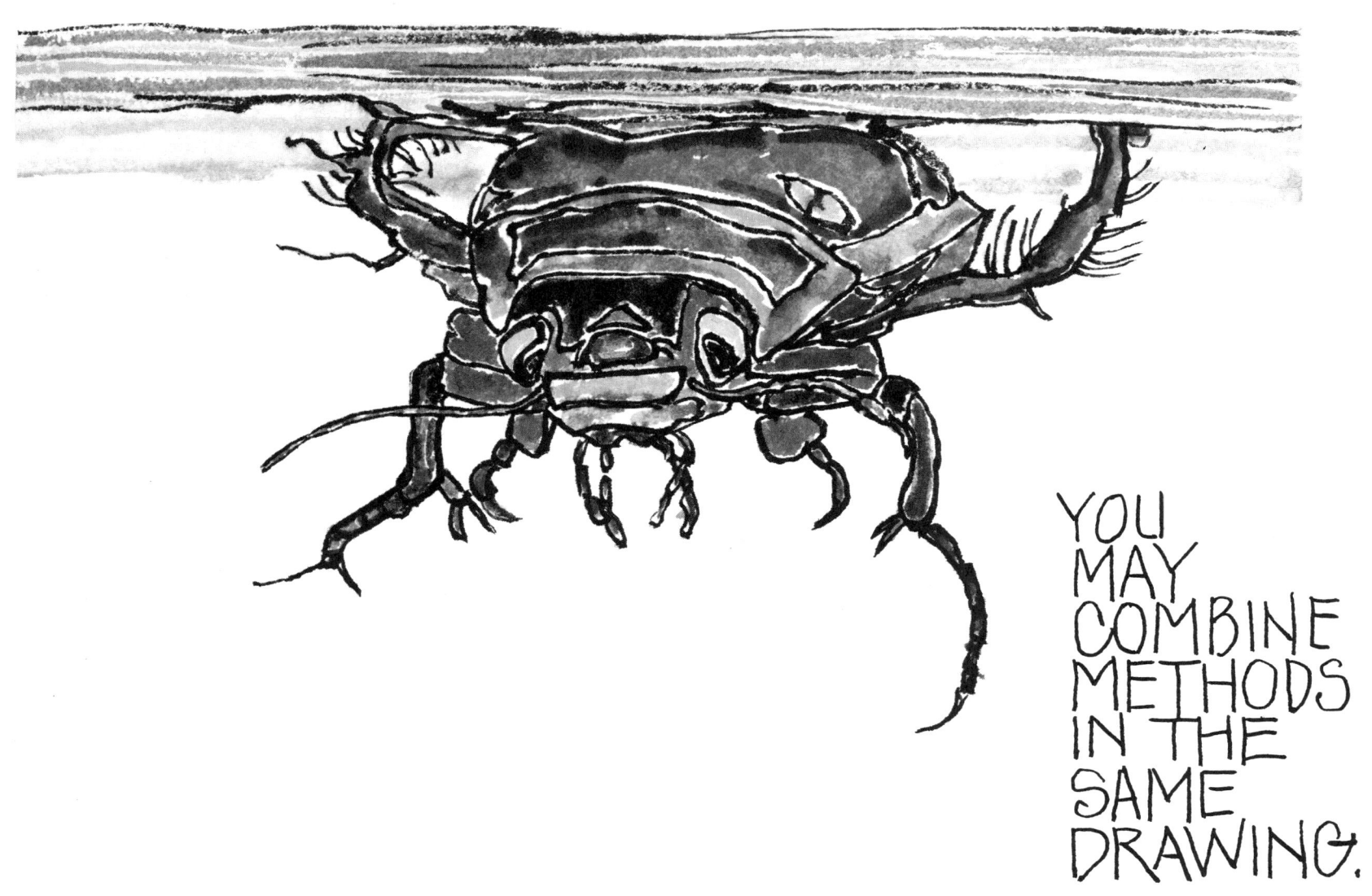

YOU MAY COMBINE METHODS IN THE SAME DRAWING.

IT TAKES ENERGY TO DO A DRAWING.

IT TAKES AWARENESS TO DO A DRAWING.

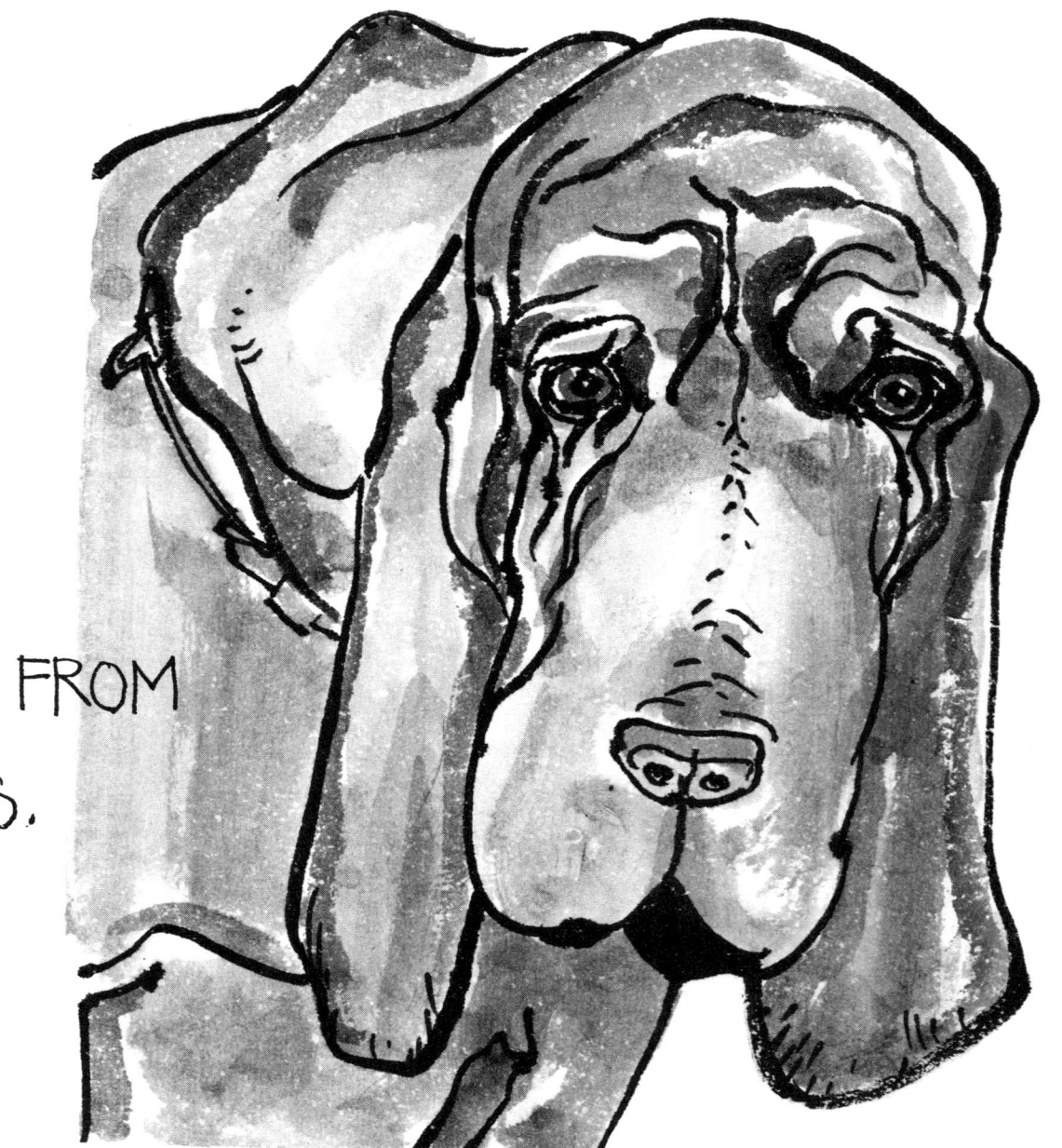

YOU CAN DRAW FROM YOUR HEART... YOUR FEELINGS.

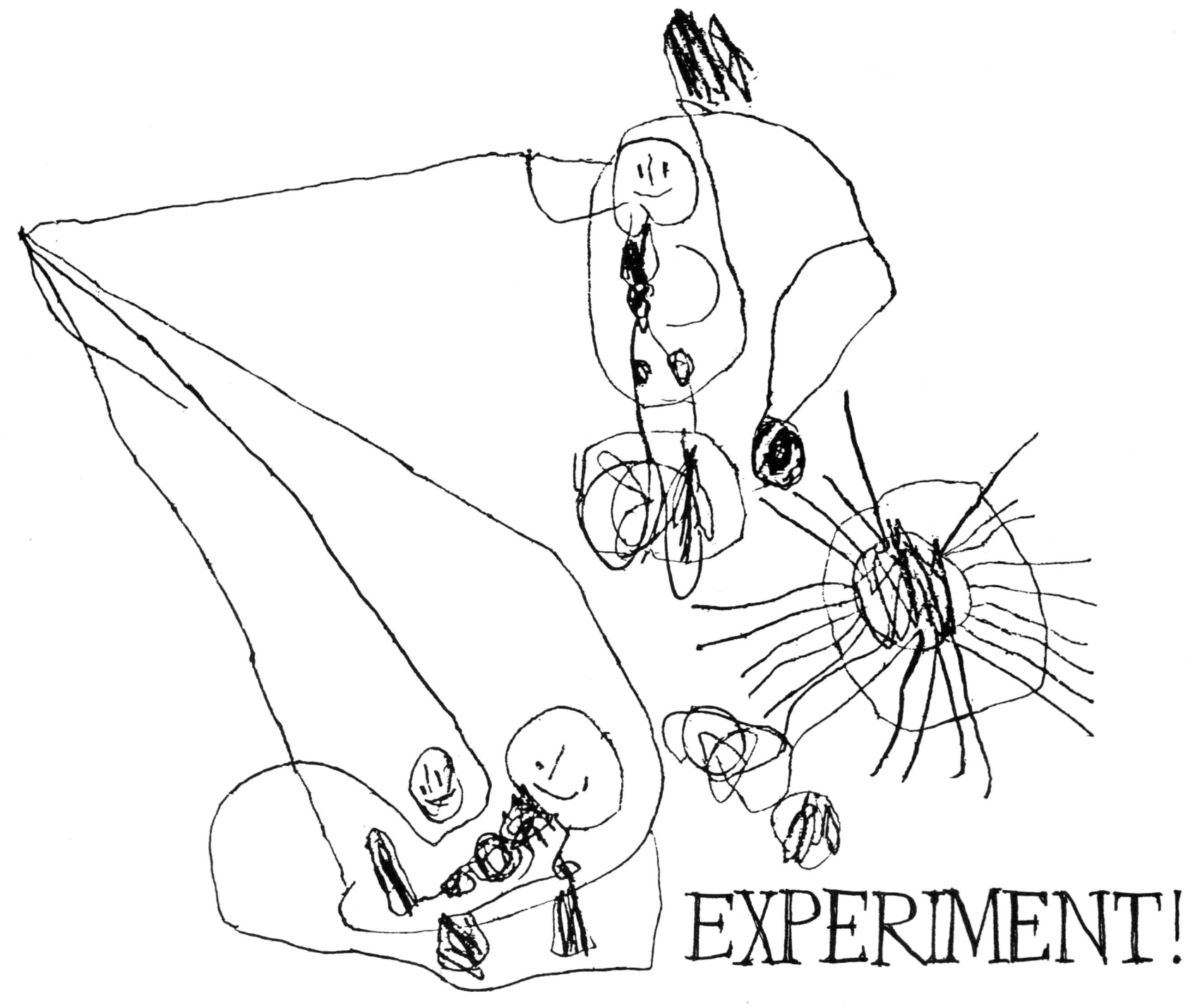

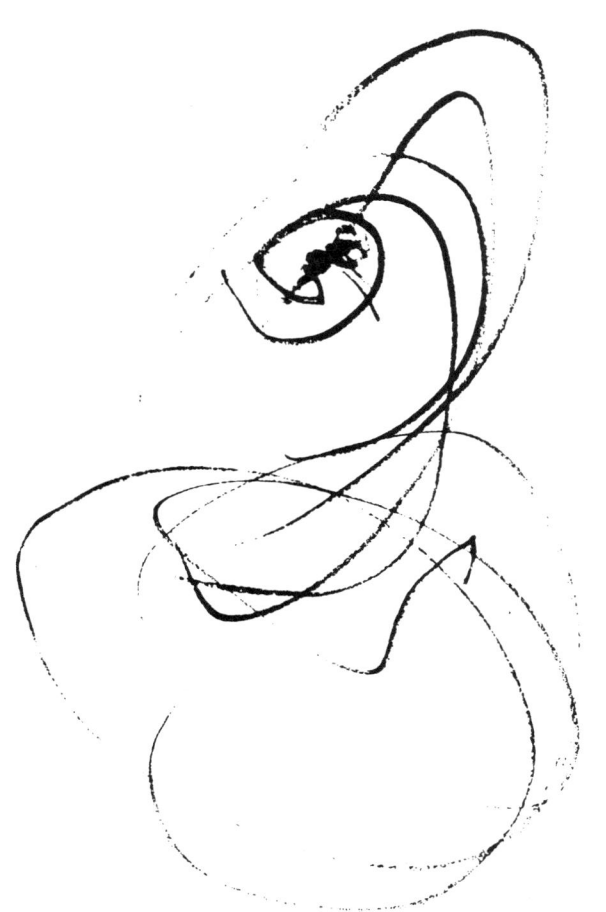

DO IT!

YOU WILL LEARN MOST BY EXPERIENCING YOURSELF DRAWING. HAVE YOUR JUDGE TAKE A WALK AND LET YOUR CREATIVE SELF PLAY.

DRAW WITH JOY, WITH GLADNESS. TAKE PLEASURE IN YOUR EXPERIENCE. DRAW WITH ENTHUSIASM! THEN MIRACLES CAN BE EXPECTED.

KEEP THE DRAWINGS THAT YOU LIKE. PUT THE DRAWINGS YOU LIKE BEST ON YOUR WALL. WHEN YOU LOOK AT THEM, REMIND YOURSELF THAT YOU MADE THEM.

WE LEARN THAT WE CAN TRANSFORM MISTAKES AND ACCIDENTS INTO OPPORTUNITIES — NEW IDEAS TO BUILD ON, NEW DIRECTIONS TO FOLLOW.

YOU CAN DISCOVER THOUSANDS OF POSSIBILITIES WHEN YOU JUST LET YOURSELF DRAW AS YOU DRAW. DON'T EXPECT YOUR DRAWINGS TO ALWAYS FIT YOUR MENTAL PICTURES. THEY MAY NOT. LET YOUR DRAWINGS BE THE WAY YOU MAKE THEM. THEY ARE PERFECT JUST LIKE THAT. THROW YOUR ERASERS AWAY. THROW THE WHITE-OUT AWAY.

KEEP THE ATTITUDE THAT EACH LINE IS FINE... JUST LIKE THAT, AND THAT, AND THAT. LET YOUR LINES BE!
DON'T TRY TO IMPROVE YOUR LINES BY GOING OVER THEM. THIS WILL MAKE YOUR LINES MUDDLED OR INDISTINCT. YOUR LINES ARE GOOD JUST THE WAY YOU MADE THEM THE FIRST TIME.

WHEN YOU FEEL THAT YOU MADE A LINE IN AN INCORRECT PLACE, LEAVE IT ALONE! SIMPLY MAKE A NEW LINE IN THE PLACE WHERE YOU FEEL IT SHOULD BE. IF THE CHANGE IS MINOR, FORGET IT. JUST LEAVE THE FIRST LINE AND LET IT BE.

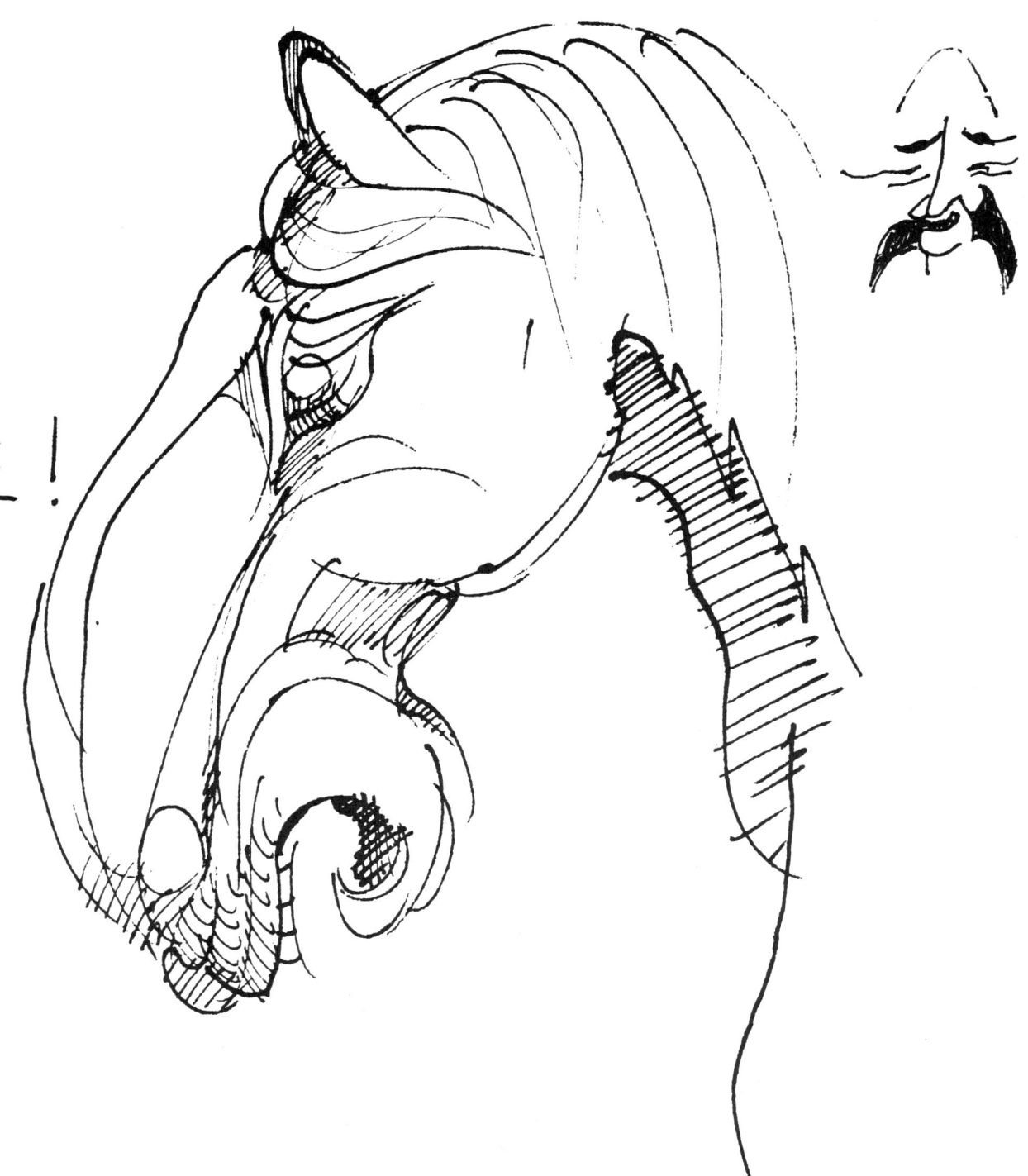

BE DECISIVE!

AS MARTIN LUTHER ONCE SAID,

"IF YOU ARE GOING TO SIN, SIN BOLDLY."

DRAW LIKE AN UNINHIBITED CHILD. LET YOUR LINES MOVE FREELY AND CONTINUOUSLY.

GET INVOLVED IN THE PROCESS OF DISCOVERING AND MAKING YOUR DRAWING.

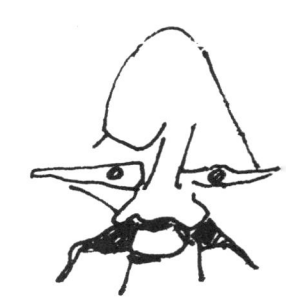
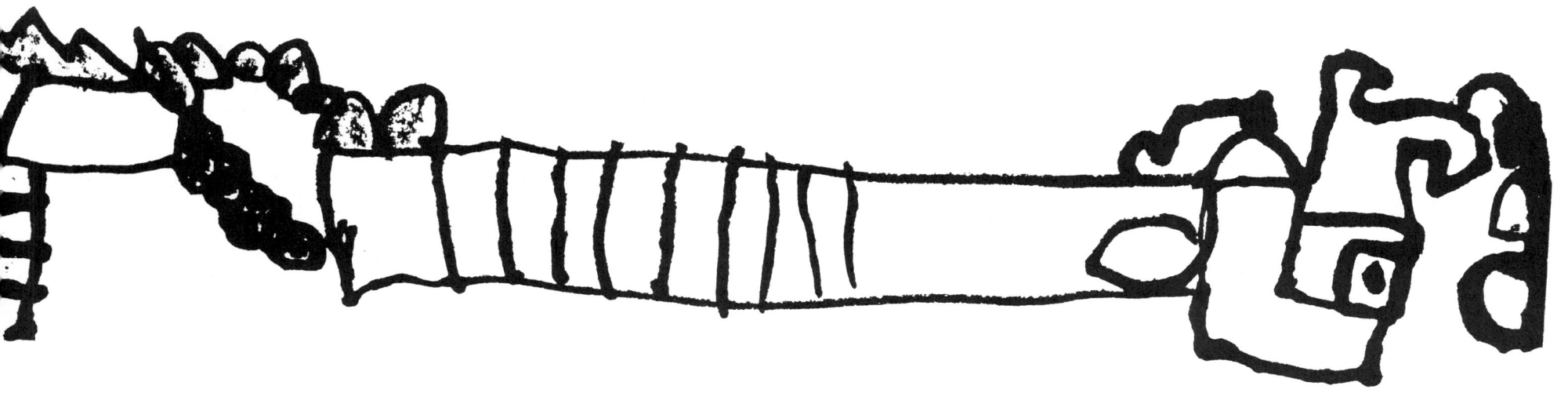

LET THE ACTIVITY ITSELF BE MOST IMPORTANT. LET GO OF YOUR CONCERN FOR THE FINISHED PRODUCT.

IT'S OKAY TO HAVE LITTLE CONCERN WITH PROPORTIONS. LET THEM VARY AND CHANGE.

LET YOUR PROPORTIONS BE THE WAY YOU MAKE THEM. CONCERN WILL TAKE AWAY FROM YOUR ABILITY TO EXPERIENCE. DON'T BE TOO CONCERNED.

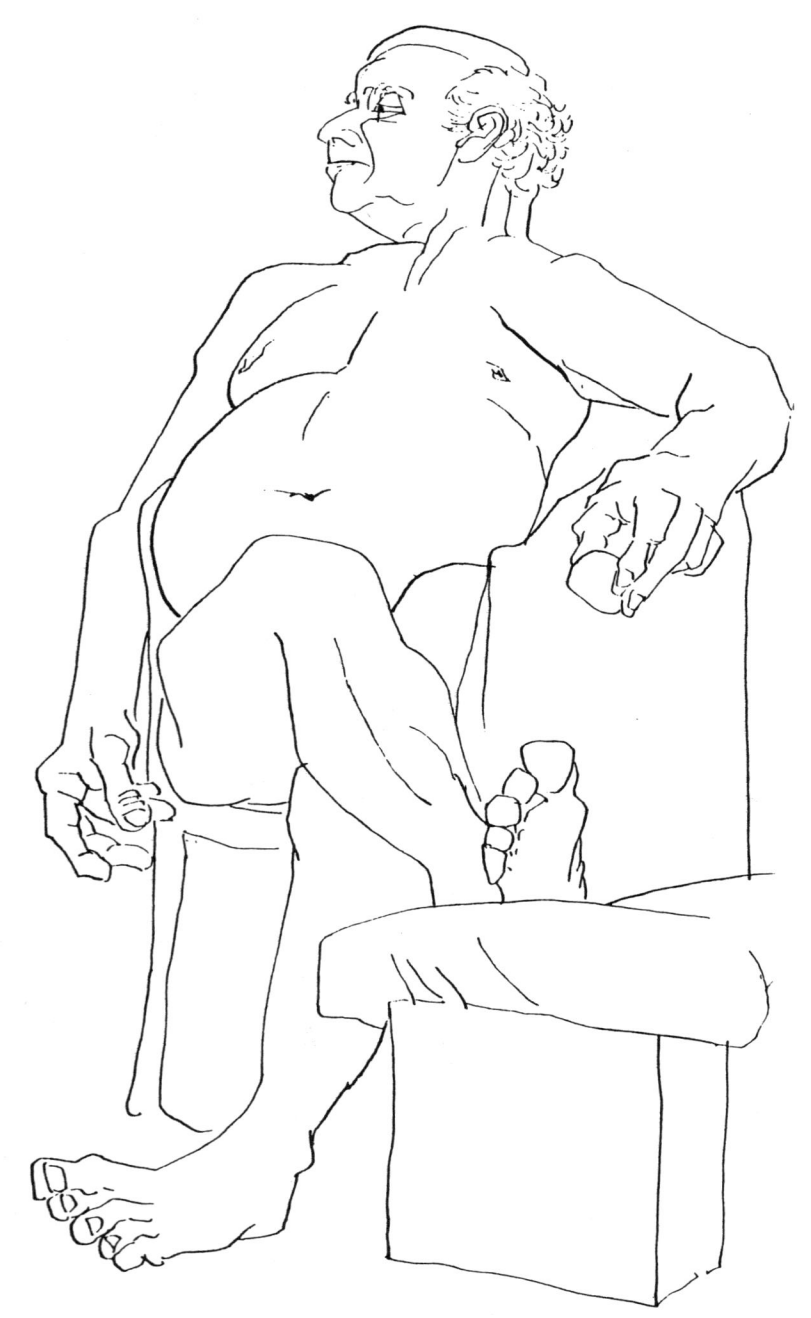

MAKE YOUR DRAWING AS EFFORTLESS AS POSSIBLE. LET YOUR DRAWINGS FLOW OUT OF YOU.

DRAW WITH CERTAINTY!

A DRAWING IS A RECORD OF YOUR EXPERIENCE...

AT THAT PLACE AND TIME.

DRAW YOUR EXPERIENCE.

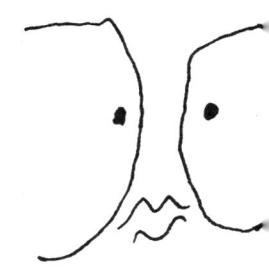

DRAWING IS AN EXPERIENCE.
WHEN YOU DRAW YOU CAN TRULY EXPERIENCE.
YOU <u>CREATE</u> EXPERIENCE.

DRAWING IS AN ADVENTURE, AN EXPLORATION INTO UNKNOWN TERRITORY. IT CAN BE RISKY. YOU DON'T KNOW WHAT A DRAWING WILL BE LIKE UNTIL YOU HAVE DONE IT. YOU MUST DO YOUR OWN EXPLORING AND MAKE YOUR OWN DISCOVERIES.

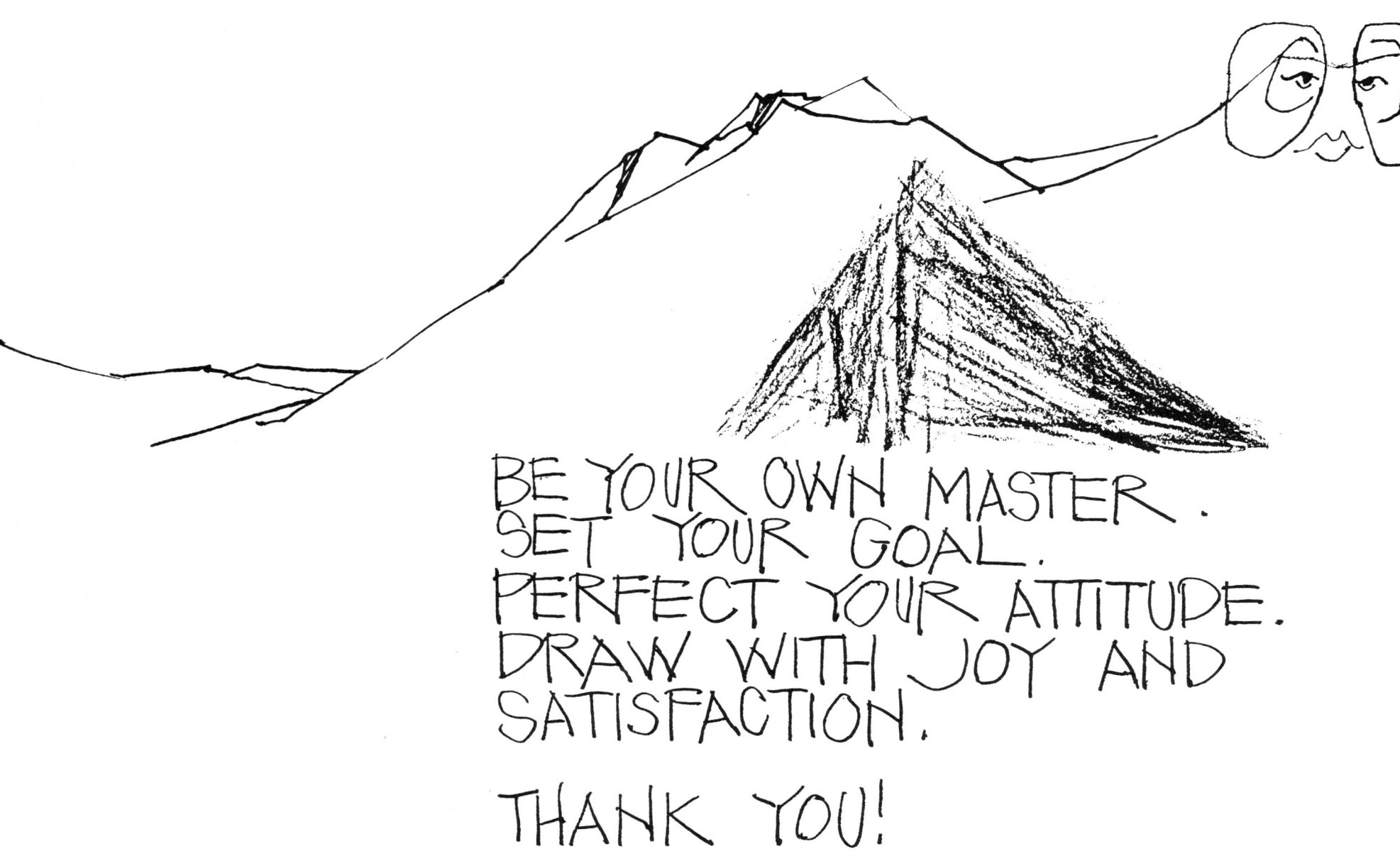

METHODS AND TOOLS

The following are methods for practicing a kind of representational and expressive drawing based upon one's experience of seeing. There are, of course, many ways to draw; this is one way.

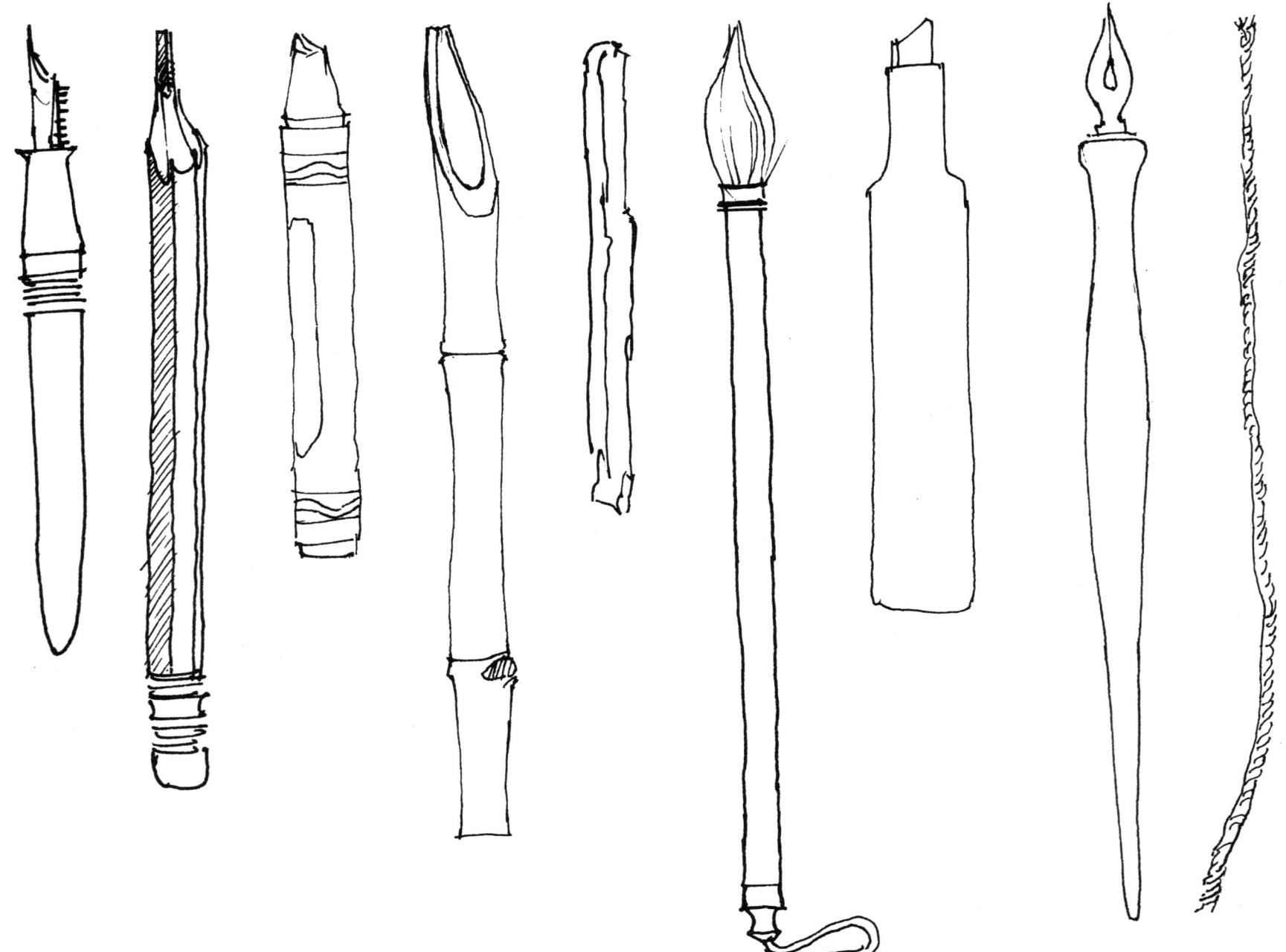

FOR THOSE WHO SIMPLY DON'T
  KNOW WHERE TO BEGIN,
  HERE IS A WAY.

FIND A DRAWING INSTRUMENT:
A PEN, A PENCIL, A CRAYON,
A BAMBOO PEN, A STICK OF
CHARCOAL, A BRUSH, A FELT TIP PEN,
A STEEL PEN, A PIECE OF STRING,
WHATEVER.

HOLD IT WITH YOUR
FINGERS
TEETH
TOES

RELAX.
STAND OR SIT
COMFORTABLY
AND
BREATHE EASILY.

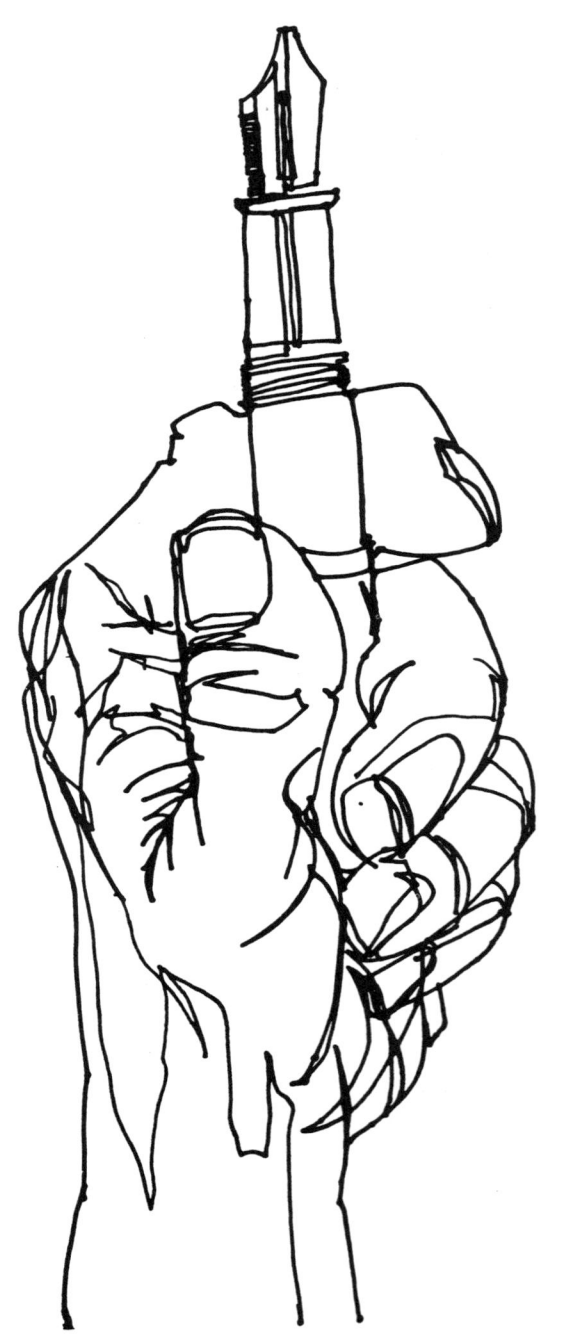

SCRIBBLE —
WITHOUT EFFORT, WITHOUT TRYING TO DRAW ANYTHING, JUST SCRIBBLE — WITH FREEDOM, WITH EASE, HAVE FUN. WATCH YOURSELF SCRIBBLE. IF YOU FEEL JUST LIKE A KID YOU ARE DOING IT RIGHT.

NOW, WITHOUT LOOKING AT YOUR PAPER, DRAW YOUR HAND (THE ONE THAT IS NOT HOLDING THE PEN). IMAGINE THAT THE POINT OF YOUR PEN AND YOUR EYE ARE CONNECTED. AS YOUR EYE MOVES AROUND THE CONTOURS OF YOUR HAND, LET THE POINT OF YOUR PEN RECORD WHAT YOU SEE. IMAGINE THAT YOUR PEN IS ACTUALLY TOUCHING YOUR SUBJECT AS YOUR EYES DISCOVER THE FORMS.

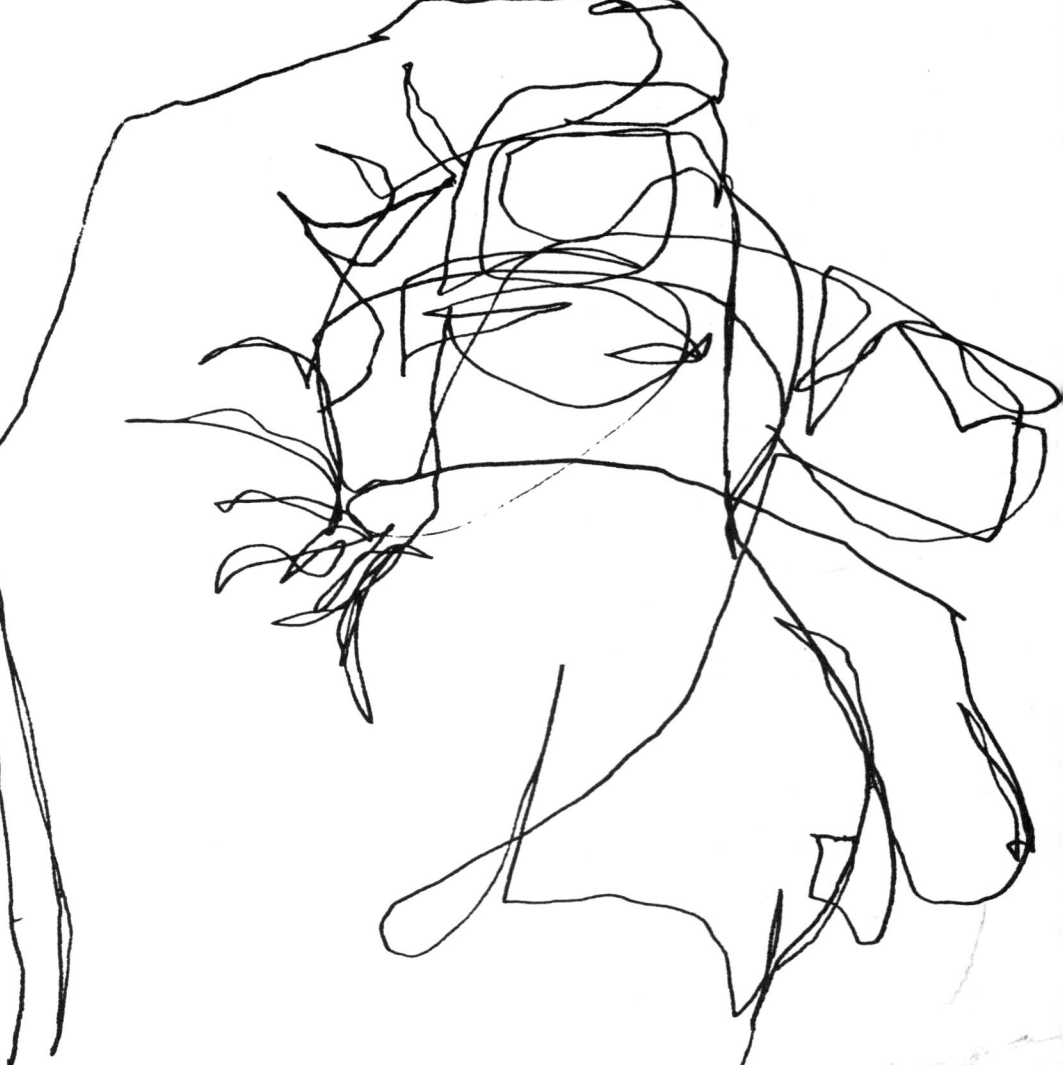

MOVE YOUR PEN AS FAST OR AS SLOW AS YOU FEEL COMFORTABLE BUT DON'T MISS ANYTHING. DRAW EVERY EDGE, WRINKLE, FINGERNAIL, ETC., WITH <u>ONE CONTINUOUS LINE</u>. IN ORDER TO ACCOMPLISH THIS IT IS O.K. TO PUT IN SOME EXTRA LINES. REMEMBER TO KEEP YOUR EYES ON YOUR SUBJECT AT ALL TIMES. RESIST THE TEMPTATION TO SEE WHAT IS HAPPENING ON THE PAPER. WAIT UNTIL YOU ARE FINISHED AND HAVE TAKEN THE PEN OFF THE PAPER BEFORE YOU LOOK. PUT YOUR HAND IN DIFFERENT POSITIONS SO THAT YOU CAN PRACTICE THIS EXERCISE TEN OR MORE TIMES IN SUCCESSION.

REMEMBER DO NOT TAKE THE PEN OFF THE PAPER UNTIL YOU HAVE DRAWN EVERY PART OF YOUR HAND THAT YOU CAN SEE FOR EACH POSITION.

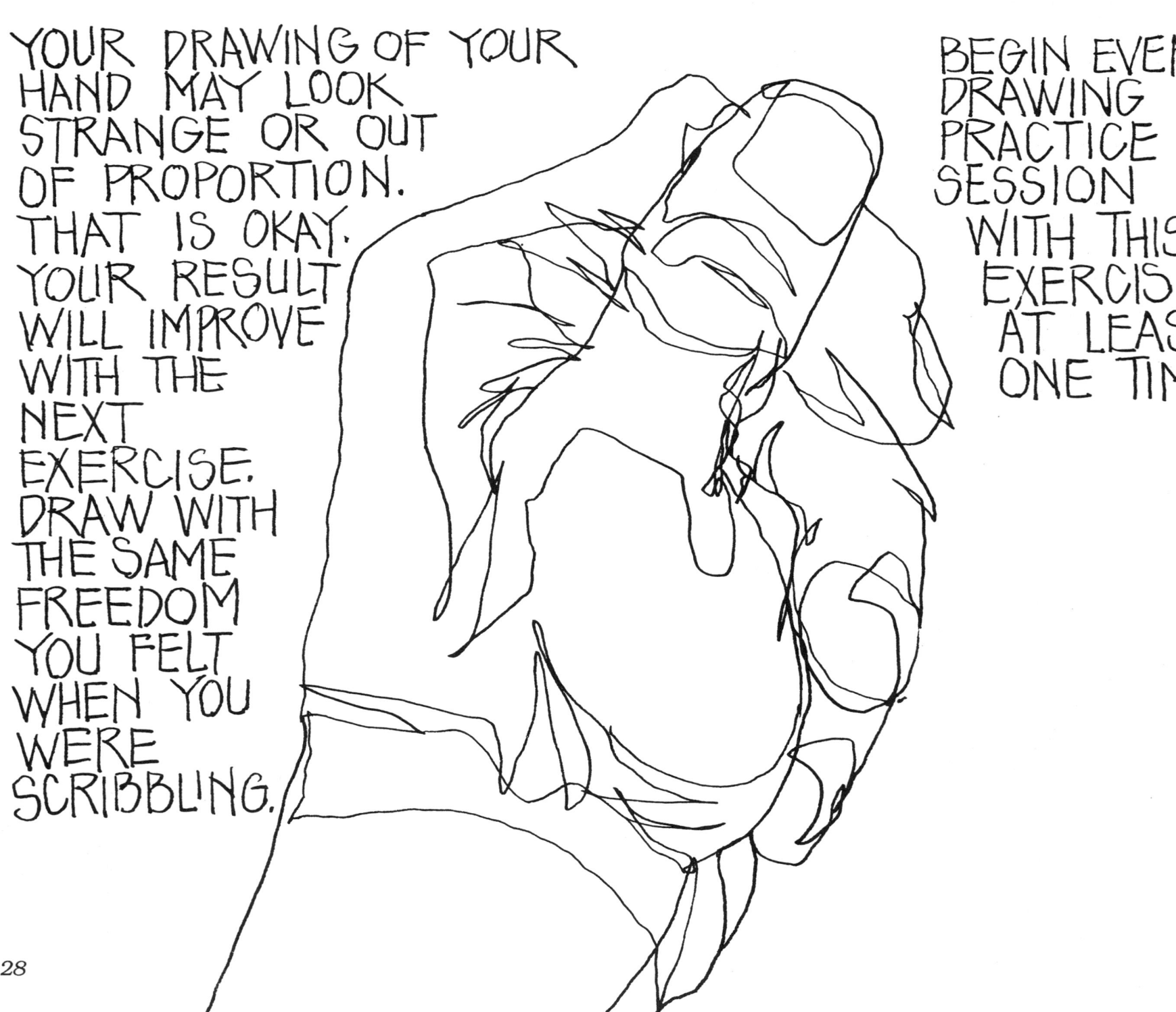

YOUR DRAWING OF YOUR HAND MAY LOOK STRANGE OR OUT OF PROPORTION. THAT IS OKAY. YOUR RESULT WILL IMPROVE WITH THE NEXT EXERCISE. DRAW WITH THE SAME FREEDOM YOU FELT WHEN YOU WERE SCRIBBLING.

BEGIN EVERY DRAWING PRACTICE SESSION WITH THIS EXERCISE AT LEAST ONE TIME.

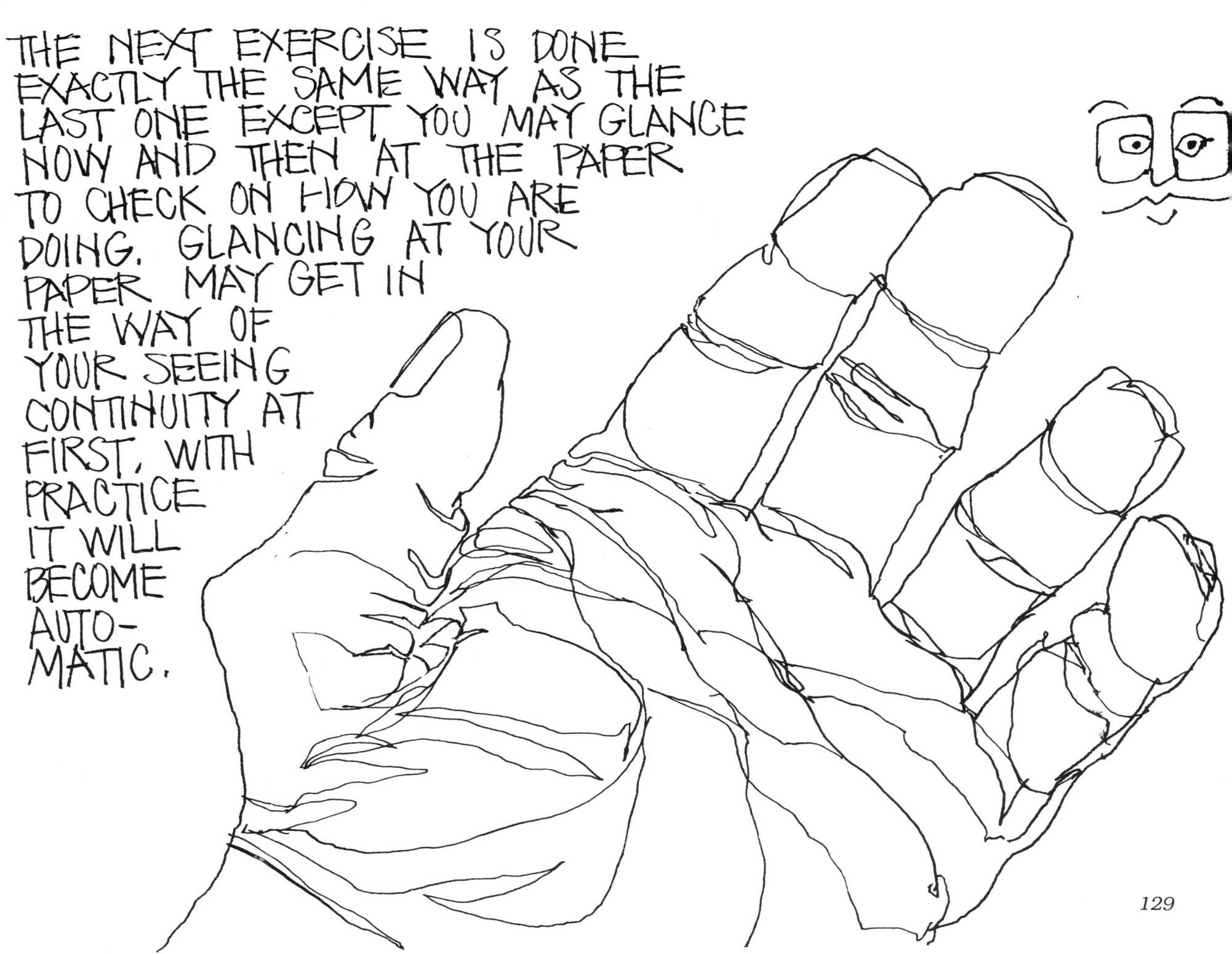

Now draw a friend's face. Do it the same way that you did the first hand drawings. Draw everything that you see. Take the time to look at your friend as thoroughly as possible. The success of your drawing depends on how well you see your subject. Remember one line only and no looking at the paper.

NOW DRAW YOUR FRIEND AGAIN. THIS TIME GLANCE AT THE PAPER FROM TIME TO TIME WHILE YOU ARE DRAWING. REMEMBER, MAKE ONLY ONE LINE FOR EACH EDGE.
SPEND MOST OF THE DRAWING TIME LOOKING AT YOUR SUBJECT, NOT AT THE PAPER. CONCENTRATE. DISCOVER. INVESTIGATE.

WHEN YOU DRAW, MAKE YOURSELF COMFORTABLE. SIT OR STAND WITH BOTH FEET ON THE FLOOR. REMEMBER TO DRAW AS LARGE AS POSSIBLE. FILL YOUR SHEET WITH YOUR SUBJECT EVEN IF IT MEANS DRAWING LARGER THAN THE SUBJECT REALLY IS. THIS WILL PROMOTE FREEDOM AND CREATIVE EXPRESSION. IF YOU ARE DRAWING IN A CLASSROOM YOU CAN DRAW EACH OTHER AT THE SAME TIME. YOU MAY EXAGGERATE OR USE DIFFERENT LINE WEIGHTS FOR EMPHASIS. EVENTUALLY YOU MAY WANT TO SEPARATE YOUR LINES,

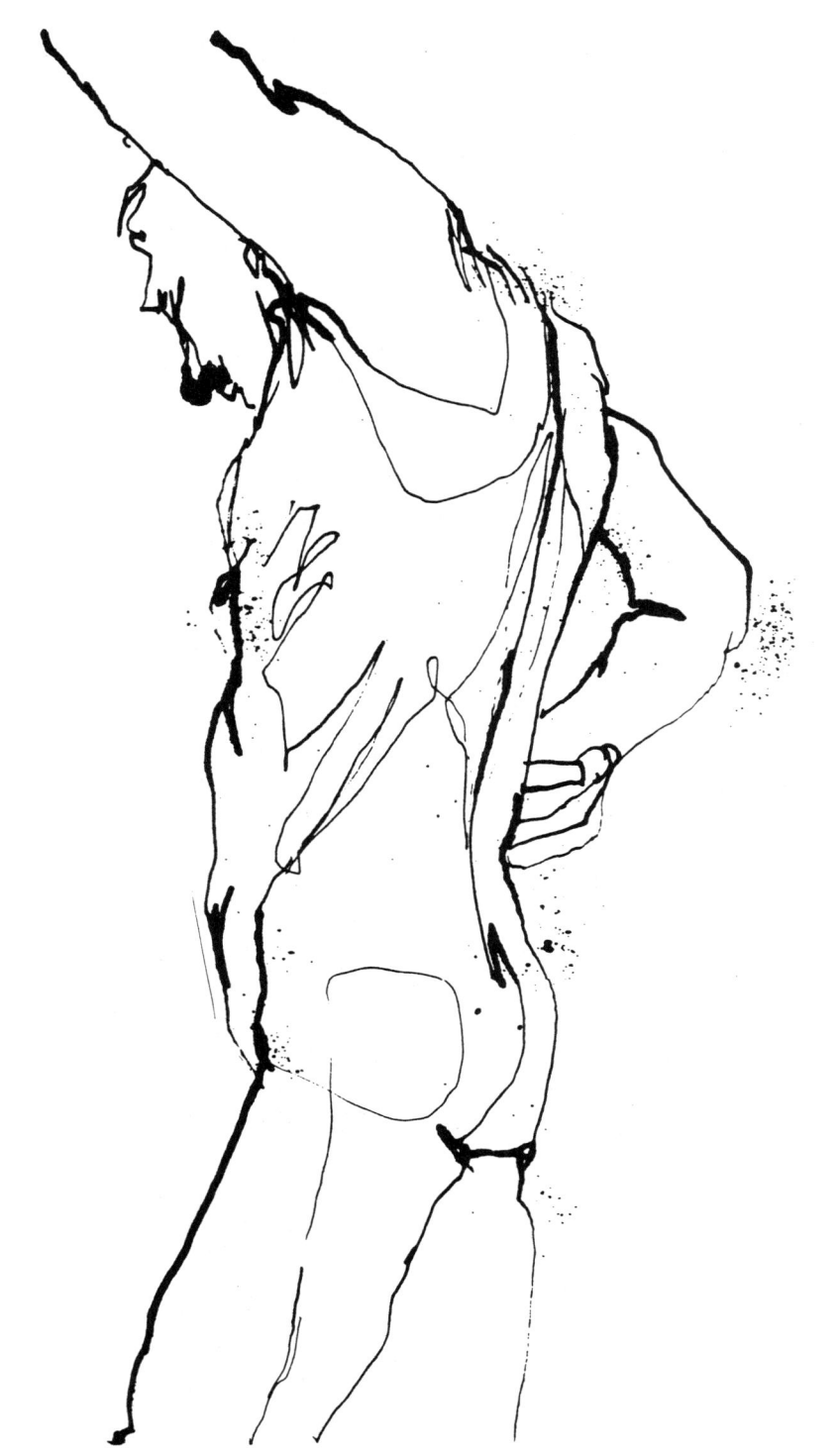

BUT THE CONTINUOUS LINE WILL ALWAYS GIVE YOUR DRAWING A WONDERFUL UNITY. YOU MAY ALSO DECIDE TO LEAVE THINGS OUT OR REARRANGE THINGS IN YOUR DRAWINGS. GO BACK AND READ OVER THE FIRST PART OF THIS BOOK TO REDISCOVER SOME OF THE MANY POSSIBILITIES.

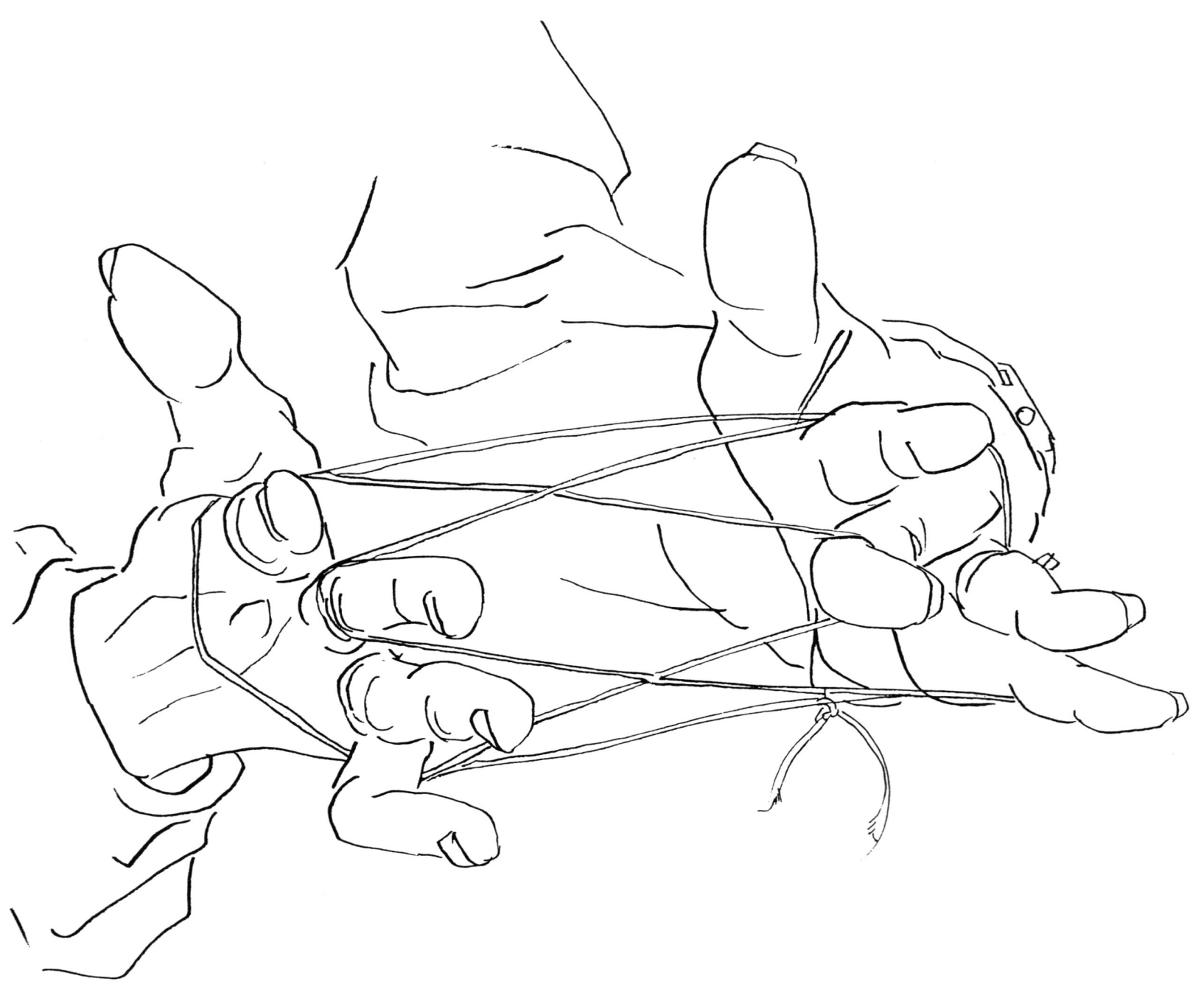

DOCUMENTATION OF DRAWINGS

All of the drawings in this book were made by the author, Robert Regis Dvořák; and his sons, Michael Edward Dvořák and David Allen Dvořák. The following is a documentation of each drawing, including the artist, the medium, and the original size. Most of the drawings were not made to be used specifically in this book but rather are works from the artists' collections. (The artists' names are abbreviated RD, Robert Regis Dvořák, MD, Michael Dvořák; DD, David Dvořák.)

All odd-numbered pages *Face Dance Sequence* (RD). Pen and ink on paper. These images were taken from an animated film by the author, titled *Face Dance*, made in 1974. It is a kinetic sketch book of 4,560 faces painted on 16 mm film. Sizes as shown.

Frontispiece *Father and Sons* (RD). Ink, dry brush drawing on oriental paper. Oriental paper is sometimes referred to as rice paper. There are many varieties of oriental paper. The oriental paper used for drawings in this book is a light white absorbent paper. This drawing was made for a commemorative poster announcing the first exhibition *Drawing Without Fear*, held at the Seipp Gallery, Castilleja School, Palo Alto, California, April 14–May 14, 1986. 19" x 28-1/2".

page 2 *Drawing Class* (RD). Marking pen on newsprint. The hand in the foreground is that of the author while he draws the concentrated students. 36" x 18".

page 3 *Spiral* (MD). Red Chinese watercolor on computer paper. 11" x 15".

page 4 *Tibetan Reed Player* (RD). Steel quill pen, black ink on oriental paper. 6" x 9".

page 5 *Beast* (MD). Black felt tip marking pen on white paper. 17" x 11".

page 6 *Unique Drawing* (MD). Black felt tip marking pen on white computer paper. 11" x 15".

page 7 *Self-Portrait with Two Birds* (MD). Black Sharpie pen on white computer paper. Michael's signature appears at the top. This drawing was a gift to his mother. Most of the boys' drawings were gifts to someone— expressions of love. 11" x 15".

page 8 *Personal Creation* (MD). Black marking pen on white paper. 9" x 12".

page 9 *Primates* (RD). Bamboo pen, black ink on Stillman sketch book paper. These two sketches were made very quickly during a visit to the San Francisco Zoo. 14" x 11".

page 10 *Man Reading* (RD). Fountain pen, black ink on cotton rag typing paper. Most of the fountain pen drawings in this book were made with an inexpensive Sheaffer pen. Page 10 contains five Pocket Drawing Pad sketches. 8-1/2" x 11".

page 11 *Cow and Her Calf* (RD). Fountain pen and black ink on white drawing paper. Driving along Skyline Boulevard in Palo Alto, California, I saw these cows, stopped the car, and made this quick sketch. Animals must be drawn quickly as they are constantly moving. 3-1/2" x 4-3/4 ".

page 12 *Design* (DD). Black Sharpie pen on white bond paper. 8-1/2" x 11".

page 13 *Little David* (RD). Steel quill pen, brush, black ink and wash on oriental paper. I made this sketch of David when he was about eighteen months old. The line drawing was made first, then the washes were added. 8" x 8".

page 14 *Spectators* (RD). Fountain pen, black ink on white bond paper. These figures were drawn at the Stedelijk Museum in Amsterdam. 11" x 8-1/2".

page 15 *Flies* (RD). Steel quill pen, black ink on scraps of rice paper. I sketched this fly one evening as it crawled around on my desk while I was working. 11" x 8-1/2".

page 16 *Sitting David* (RD). Mechanical drafting pen on Stillman sketch book paper. 14" x 11".

page 17 *Woman* (RD). Steel quill pen, black ink, brush on white paper. This was a demonstration drawing I made for a class. The project was to draw a face of another person in the class but to exaggerate the width by drawing it on a half sheet of sketch book paper. 5-1/2" x 14".

page 18 *Lion* (RD). Steel quill pen, black ink on oriental paper. This quick sketch was made at the San Francisco Zoo. 5-1/2" x 9-3/4".

page 19 *Untitled* (RD). Chinese ink, brush on rice paper. 13" x 9-1/2".

page 20 *Old Woman in Venice* (RD). Mechanical drafting pen on Fabriano paper. This woman was sitting across from me. I could not resist doing this drawing. It's perfect. 9-1/2" x 6-3/4".

page 21 *Flying Something* (MD). Black felt tip pen on white paper. 11" x 16".

page 22 *Bear* (RD). Bamboo pen, black ink on Stillman sketch book paper. A one-minute sketch made at the San Francisco Zoo. 14" x 11".

page 23 *Pandas* (RD). Fountain pen, black ink on Pentalic sketch book paper. A very quick sketch of the panda bears at the zoo in Cheng Du, China. The black areas were filled in later on the tour bus. 5-1/2" x 8-1/2 ".

pages 24 & 25 *Roots* (RD). Chinese ink on oriental paper (cropped). The upper Vernal Falls area in Yosemite inspired this drawing on a long sheet of rice paper that I carried with me. 9" x 48".

page 26 *Cat* (RD). Bamboo pen and black ink wash on light tan rag paper. 10" x 8-3/4".

page 27 *Design* (MD). Black felt tip pen on white bond typing paper. 8 12/" x 11". *Barge* (RD). Fountain pen on Pentalic sketch book paper. The barge drawing was made on the lower Yangtze River as I stood at the railing of a passenger ferry. 5-1/2" x 8-1/2".

page 28 *Woman* (RD). Steel quill pen, black ink on Stillman sketch book paper. 14" x 11".

page 29 *Old Jalopy* (RD). Pelikan font ink, fountain pen on tracing vellum. With my eyes closed, I imagined an old jalopy and then drew it with one continuous line without opening my eyes until I was finished. 12" x 16".

page 30 *Inner World* (RD). Colored wax crayons, water color dyes on white paper. 12" x 18".

page 31 *Beach People* (RD). Fountain pen, black ink on white cotton rag paper. These quick loose sketches were made at the beach at Half Moon Bay in California on a Sunday afternoon. 8-1/2" x 11".

page 32 *Hippo* (RD). Steel quill pen, black ink on oriental paper. Here is an example of how you can say a lot with very little. This is the easy way to draw a hippopotamus. 6" x 12-1/4".

page 33 *Waterfalls* (RD). Calligraphy pen, black ink on white cotton rag paper. 11" x 8-1/2".

page 34 *Untitled* (MD). Pencil on white typing paper. 8-1/2" x 11".

page 35 *Tahoe Tree* (RD). Chinese ink, brush, bamboo pen on white oriental paper. This very large drawing was made from a smaller sketch. Can you see the two crows in the tree? And the mouse near the roots? 72" x 36".

page 36 *Pitcher* (RD). Pencil on white drawing paper. This pewter pitcher was drawn carefully and slowly as a demonstration drawing. It lacks life and emotion and is not my kind of drawing. 11" x 14".

page 37 *Ink Blot Face* (RD). Chinese ink, brush on white drawing paper. The other ink blot drawing in this book is on page 52. The technique is simple: Fold the paper, with a brush or pen create your image on one side of the paper, and fold to transfer while it is still wet. I recommend that the blotting be done after each stroke. 12" x 18".

page 38 *Pat* (RD). Chinese ink, brush on oriental paper. I sketched Pat, a friend, during a Sunday afternoon visit. 12" x 16".

page 39 *Untitled* (MD). Colored felt tip pens on computer paper. 8" x 6".

page 40 *Skopolos* (RD). Chinese ink, brush on oriental paper. I sketched this scene after lunch while sitting at an outdoor restaurant on this Greek island. This was the spectacular view from my chair. 12" x 19".

page 41 *Kitten* (MD). Chinese ink, brush on oriental paper. 11" x 15".

page 42 *Shoes* (RD). Bamboo pen and fountain pen, black India ink. This is a part of a larger drawing of my sons' shoes next to one of mine. 10" x 24".

page 43 *Floating Soft Mechanical Contraption* (RD). Fountain pen, black ink on white bond— a composite. I doodled this while waiting for a movie to begin. 8-1/2" x 11".

pages 44 & 45 *Long Drawing* (DD, RD). Felt tip pen composite. This wonderful sketch, made by my son David on a scrap of paper he found on the floor, was so free and imaginative that I decided to use it for the cover of this book. These pages show how the original sketch looked— reduced in size of course. My men were added for fun. 4" x 33-1/2".

page 46 *Giraffes* (RD). Bamboo pen, black ink on Stillman sketch book paper. These magnificent animals were sketched at the San Francisco Zoo. 14" x 11".

page 47 *Rooster* (RD). Fountain pen, black ink on an index card. This Pocket Drawing Pad drawing was made at the Children's Zoo in the San Francisco Zoo. 6" x 4".

page 48 *Venice Church* (RD). Mechanical drafting pen, black ink on rag card stock. This continuous line sketch, shown actual size, was drawn in seconds. 4-1/2" x 3-1/2".

page 49 *Strawberry* (RD). Chinese brush, ink on rice paper. 18" x 14".

page 50 *Birds* (RD). Calligraphy pen, black ink on card stock. You can say a lot with so very little. It took less than a minute to record these pigeons in the Piazza San Marco, Venice. 4-1/2" x 3-1/2 ".

page 51 *Spark Plug* (RD). Fountain pen, black ink on white cotton rag paper. Everyday objects can become valuable studies. 11" x 8-1/2".

page 52 *Butterfly* (RD). Chinese brush, black ink on white drawing paper, ink blot transfer. Another ink blot drawing. See the documentation for page 37 for a more specific explanation. 12" x 18".

page 53 *Story* (DD). Pencil on white paper. It is fascinating to hear what children had in mind while they drew. In this case David's mother made notes on the drawing as he talked. 11" x 8-1/2".

page 54 *Holland, Leaning Tower* (RD). Steel quill pen, ink and ink wash on oriental paper. The dramatic sky was really there. In fact, I had just finished the drawing when a terrific rain began and I had to scramble for some shelter on the leeward side of the bridge from which I made the sketch. Rain storms come and go quickly in Holland and in ten minutes the rain stopped. My drawing got a bit wet despite my efforts to keep it dry. I placed it on the side of the bridge to dry in the sun. Suddenly a wind blew my drawing pad into the creek. I quickly fished it out and here the drawing survives. 11" x 15".

page 55 *The Acropolis* (RD). Mechanical drafting pen, black ink on tracing vellum. 11" x 8-1/2".

page 56 *Flower and Fly* (RD). Bamboo pen, black ink on Stillman sketch book paper. Draw not just a flower but your hand holding a flower. 14" x 11".

page 57 *Fall Trees* (RD). Bamboo pen and steel quill pen, black ink wash on buff paper. I set a time limit for this drawing: ten minutes. Limiting your drawing time can help you loosen up. 8" x 10".

page 58 *Picasso* (RD). Chinese fountain pen, black ink on white cotton rag paper. A drawing of a man who knew how to draw without fear. 11" x 8-1/2".

page 59 *Waterfalls* (RD). Calligraphy fountain pen, black ink on white cotton rag paper. 11" x 8-1/2".

page 60 *Flying Machine* (MD). Colored felt tip pens on computer paper. 11" x 15".

page 61 *Characters* (RD). Bamboo pen, black ink on Stillman sketch book paper. The technique used here is to make a loose free line and then see what you can turn it into. 14" x 11".

pages 62 & 63 *Floating Bok Choy* (RD). Chinese ink and Chinese watercolor on rice paper. This vegetable looks almost like some kind of strange fish. 12" x 32".

page 64 *Central Greece* (RD). Chinese fountain pen, black ink on sketch paper (cropped). This drawing was made as I was looking out of a bus window. It is not easy to draw on a moving bus. However, you should draw whenever you are inspired, no matter what the circumstances. 5-1/2" x 16".

page 65 *My Mother's Hands* (RD). Chinese fountain pen, black ink on sketch paper. I asked my mother to pose for me. When she came down, she had fixed her hair and was looking very nice. I told her that all I wanted to do was draw her hands. For me these hands tell the whole story— all the dishes, the diapers, the letters, her dedication to her husband and her church, playing the organ at church and the piano at home. Her hands, now severely arthritic, testify to a life well lived. 11" x 14".

page 66 *Space Ship Under Water* (DD). Black Sharpie pen on white bond paper. 11" x 8-1/2".

page 67 *Yosemite Cliffs* (RD). Bamboo pen, black India ink on Arches watercolor paper. 8-1/2" x 4".

page 68 *Left Hand* (RD). Bamboo pen, black ink on drawing paper. 14" x 11".

page 69 *John* (RD). Bamboo stick, black ink on drawing paper. I like to draw older faces because of the character lines. Faces tell a story like hands do. You can "read" a face. 14" x 11".

page 70 *Orchids* (RD). Fountain pen, black ink on drawing paper. When I saw these orchids at a friend's house, I asked for drawing paper, which was happily provided. Sometimes the urge to draw takes preference over everything else. 10-1/2" x 21".

page 71 *Road Less Traveled* (RD). Fountain pen, black ink on white oriental paper. "I shall be telling this with a sigh/Somewhere ages and ages hence:/Two roads diverged in a wood, and I— /I took the one less traveled by,/And that has made all the difference" (from "The Road Not Taken" by Robert Frost). Not everyone wants to draw but those who do find great rewards. 6" x 5".

page 72 *Belly Dancer* (RD). Fountain pen, black ink on white rag paper. The wiggling, giggling, free lines in this drawing seem to go well with the motion of this belly dancer sketched during a demonstration performance. She was dancing with a jar balanced on her head. 11" x 8-1/2".

page 73 *Karl* (RD). Drafting pens on white paper. This drawing of Karl Dohnal, an outdoorsman, was done for his book, *Yukon Solo*, published by Binford and Mort, Portland, Oregon. A pencil drawing was first made and then traced. 10-1/2" x 12-1/2".

page 74 *Design* (DD). Felt tip pens on paper. What I like about this drawing is the obvious spontaneity combined with a careful drawing method. 8-1/2" x 11".

page 75 *Crab* (RD). Chinese ink and watercolor on rice paper. Made from a photograph of a crab swimming just under the surface of the water. A definitive drawing was made and then the color was added. 12" x 12".

pages 76 & 77 *Samarian Gorge* (RD). Dry brush, Chinese ink on oriental paper. This sketch of the Samarian Gorge in Crete was made from a lookout during an eight-mile hike. It was made in less than twenty minutes on a long piece of rice paper that I carried with me. The dry brush is just as fast as pencil but has the advantage of being permanent. 8" x 30".

page 78 *Bloodhound* (RD). Brush, Chinese ink and watercolor on oriental paper. 12" x 12".

page 79 *Spiral* (MD). Black felt tip marking pen on computer paper. Another spiral drawing by Michael. Michael and I have never discussed spirals. 11" x 15".
Two Chickens (RD). Fountain pen on sketch paper. The chickens were drawn at the monastery on the island of Ios, Greece. 3-1/2" x 4-3/4".

page 80 *Fred's Hand* (RD). Chinese fountain pen, black ink on white sketch paper. 11" x 14".

page 81 *Orchid* (RD). Fountain pen, black ink on heavy cotton paper. 21" x 15".

page 82 *Two Brothers* (DD). Graphite pencil on white bond paper. 11" x 8-1/2".

page 83 *Train Engine* (MD). Felt tip pen on white bond paper. 9" x 12".

page 84 *Flower Vase* (MD). Brush, watercolor on oriental paper. The flowers were drawn for a demonstration at a flower drawing workshop. 18" x 14".

page 85 *Arlan* (RD). Bamboo pen on newsprint. Two or three minutes is all the time needed to capture the essence of the figure. The bamboo pen is one of my favorite drawing instruments. 24" x 18".

page 86 *Joe* (RD). Fountain pen, black ink on sketch paper. I made this sketch of Joe as he told a story to our group during my stay in Greece. 4-3/4" x 3-1/2".

page 87 *Bridal Veil Falls* (RD). Fountain pen, black ink on 100% rag paper. Hatching lines are a good way to represent the angular rocks on a cliff. 11" x 8-1/2".

page 88 *Man* (RD). Bamboo pen, ink on sketch pad paper. 17" x 14".

page 89 *Funny Animals* (RD). Ink spots, fountain pen, black ink on paper. Drops of ink can be transformed into funny animals. A mistake can often be turned into an opportunity to try something new. Size as shown.

page 90 The lettering in this book was done freehand, without any guidelines, to be consistent with the spontaneity of drawing.

page 91 *Dad and Mom* (MD). Graphite pencil on scrap paper. 11" x 15". *Dog* (RD). Fountain pen on sketch paper. 4-1/2" x 3-3/4".

page 92 *Maze* (DD). Colored felt tip pens on white paper. 8-1/2" x 11".

page 94 *Leg* (RD). Fountain pen, black ink on Stillman sketch book paper. 14" x 11".

page 95 *Horse* (RD). Fountain pen, black ink on paper. The sketch of the horse's head was drawn from a Chinese ceramic piece at the Asian Art Museum in San Francisco. 11" x 8-1/2".

page 96 *Design* (MD). Black felt tip marking pen on white bond paper. 8-1/2" x 11".

page 97 *Walt* (RD). Three-foot stick, black ink on paper. The three-foot bamboo stick is an excellent way to loosen up a tight drawing hand. Put the paper and ink on the floor and stand over it. Dip the stick into the ink, being careful not to spill it, and draw while standing, holding onto the other end of the stick. 14" x 18".

pages 98 & 99 *Long Landscape* (DD). Black and colored marking pens on oriental paper. 3-3/4" x 30".

page 100 *Trevor* (RD). Three-foot stick, black ink on white sketch paper. 24" x 18".

page 101 *Design* (MD). Thin black felt tip pen on white bond paper. 8-1/2" x 11".

page 102 *Figure* (RD). Bamboo pen, black ink on newsprint. 8-1/2" x 11".

page 103 *Elephant* (RD). Fountain pen, black ink on oriental paper. Elephants are great subjects to draw—they are so big and round. They do move around a lot, so you must be quick to capture their form. This one was drawn at the zoo in San Francisco. 9" x 12".

page 104 *Joe* (RD). Chinese fountain pen, black ink on sketch pad paper. This drawing was made during my Monday night drawing class. We frequently have cookies on hand, and Joe was holding one as he posed for us. 24" x 18".

page 105 *House* (MD). Brush, watercolor on white butcher paper. The tall house is a frequent subject in Michael's drawings. See also page 91. 14" x 11".

page 106 *Student* (RD). Brush, Chinese black ink on oriental paper. I made this sketch of a student during one of Paul Hau's Chinese painting classes. She was watching him demonstrate a technique. 23" x 15".

page 107 *Walt* (RD). Brush, black ink on paper. I like the disproportionate hands in this drawing. 24" x 18".

page 108 *Dead Tree* (RD). Bamboo pen and steel quill pen, black ink on oriental paper. 16" x 14".

page 109 *Eyes* (MD). Chinese brush, black ink on white paper. One of my favorite drawings. 12" x 18".

pages 110 & 111 *Nuenen, Holland* (RD). Calligraphy pen, black ink on tan Reives paper. This drawing of Holland was done on an overcast day when I was feeling miserable and uncomfortable. I had broken my left hand a few days before. Since I draw right-handed most of the time, I was not greatly handicapped. I forgot my discomforts as I drew. 7" x 24".

pages 112 & 113 *Wayne's Barn* (RD). Brush, Chinese black ink on oriental paper. Old barns offer great material for drawing. Not only do they have a lot of interest and character, but they sit still. 11-1/2" x 46".

pages 114 & 115 *Michael Sleeping* (RD). Brush, Chinese black ink on oriental paper. When my son Michael was three, he was so active that the only chance to catch him long enough to draw him was while he was asleep. Here he takes an afternoon nap with his clothes on. 21-1/4" x 26".

page 116 *Monk* (RD). Steel quill pen, black ink on rice paper. Even the ink drippings can add to a drawing. 19" x 6".

page 117 *Landscape* (MD). Graphite pencil on white bond paper. This drawing reminds me of Midwestern farms as seen from the air. 8-1/2" x 11".

page 118 *Orchid* (RD). Fountain pen, black ink on heavy rag paper. 21" x 15-1/2".

page 119 *Mountain* (RD). Fountain pen, black ink on white bond paper. A mountain is a good metaphor for a personal challenge and accomplishment. The joys of satisfaction are experienced when we do something that we have never done before. A new challenge is never faced without the fear of failure. 8-1/2" x 11".

page 120 *Mykonos* (RD). Chinese fountain pen, black ink on sketch pad paper. 5-1/2" x 16".

page 122 *Drawing Instruments* (RD). Fountain pen, black ink on white rag paper. 8-1/2" x 11".

page 124 *Left Hand Holding Pen* (RD). Black Sharpie pen on newsprint. 24" x 18".

page 125 *Scribble* (RD). Black Sharpie pen on white rag paper. When scribbling you should be relaxed and not try to draw anything. Just make a mess. Move the drawing instrument any way you like. Do anything that feels like scribbling. 8-1/2" x 11".

page 126 *Hand* (RD). Fountain pen, black ink on white rag paper. 8-1/2" x 11".

page 127 *Hand (Detail)* (RD). Bamboo pen, black ink on newsprint. 24" x 18".

page 128 *Hand* (RD). Fountain pen, black ink on white rag paper. 8-1/2" x 11".

page 129 *Left Hand* (RD). Fountain pen, black ink on white rag paper. 8-1/2" x 11".

page 130 *Untitled* (RD). Black Sharpie pen on rice paper. 17-1/2" x 14-1/2".

page 131 *Woman* (RD). Steel quill pen, black ink on oriental paper. 17-1/2" x 14-1/2".

page 132 *Student* (RD). Steel quill pen, black ink on oriental paper. 17-1/2" x 14".

page 133 *Man* (RD). Bamboo pen, black ink on newsprint. The friction of the pen on the paper sometimes causes the ink to spatter. The spatters in this drawing give it an added texture. 24" x 18".

page 134 *Traveler* (RD). Fountain pen, black ink on white rag paper. 4-3/4" x 3-1/2". *Trees* (RD). Fountain pen, black ink on white rag paper. 3-1/2" x 4-3/4".

page 135 *Bird* (RD). Fountain pen, black ink on white rag paper. 8-1/2" x 11".

page 136 *Cat's Cradle* (RD). Chinese fountain pen on sketch pad paper. This ten-minute drawing was made from a live model during my Monday night class. The model's fingers were really bent as they are drawn. You can gain so much pleasure and satisfaction from just a few minutes. 24" x 18".

To order copies of Drawing Without Fear or any of Dvořák's other books directly from Inkwell Press please send a check or money order to the address below or telephone your order with a VISA or MasterCard. Call toll free: (888) YOU-DRAW.

Drawing Without Fear	$18.95
The Magic of Drawing	16.95
The Pocket Drawing Book and Pad	12.95
Experiential Drawing	16.95
The Artist's Drawing Pad 6X9 (a sketch book)	6.95
California Residents add 8.25% State Sales Tax	(0.825 tax)
Shipping for each order under $20	4.00
Each $10 over $20 add	2.00

Wholesale orders welcome. Ask about quantity discounts. If you would like to receive a catalog of other books and posters that are published by Inkwell Press, write to: Inkwell Press, PO Box 37031, Montara, CA 94037.

California artist Robert Regis Dvořák presents workshops and speeches on creativity and drawing for corporations, associations, and schools. He has been honored with one-man shows of his paintings, prints, and films in the USA, Canada and Japan. He has taught drawing to adults and children for 25 years. He taught drawing and architectural design at the University of Oregon for seven years and at the University of California, Berkeley for two years, and has taught drawing and watercolor painting through University Extensions and Community Colleges in California and Hawaii since 1978. He holds degrees in Architecture from the University of Illinois and the University of California, Berkeley, and is a Fellow of the American Academy in Rome. His workshops promote personal awareness and creative thinking. His drawing books include: *Drawing Without Fear, Experiential Drawing, The Magic of Drawing,* and *The Pocket Drawing Book,* all available from Inkwell Press.